WOMEN

IN THE CHURCH

by
Everett Ferguson

Yeomen Press
110 Meadowdale Dive
Chickasha, OK 73018

WOMEN IN THE CHURCH
ISBN 0-9663531-2-9

Copyright 2003
by Yeomen Press
110 Meadowdale Dive
Chickasha, Oklahoma 73018

Contents

1
NEW TESTAMENT TEXTS

2
EVIDENCE FROM HISTORY

Contents

3
DOCTRINAL CONSIDERATIONS

INTRODUCTION

This study attempts to apply to the question of the role of women in the assembly of the church a methodology for dealing with disputed questions of Christian practice that I previously employed in reference to instrumental music in the church[1] and to the day for observing the Lord's supper.[2] This methodology involves three steps.

(1) A careful exegesis of relevant New Testament texts. This step attempts to learn as much as one can from statements in the New Testament itself and then to put the information together in a systematic way.

(2) An examination of the historical context of the New Testament and of the early Christian development after the New Testament. This step considers what was possible in the first century and how the New Testament information is to be understood in its historical setting. Then it examines the evidence in early Christian literature outside the New Testament. This testimony from history is a control on whether one has read the Biblical texts accurately and put them together correctly. The early Christian development is a witness to the apostolic teaching and practice and must be derivable in some way from it even when it departs from it.

(3) A consideration of the doctrinal significance and coherence of the conclusions reached from the Biblical and historical evidence. An examination of whether there is theological meaning in the ascertained practices either ascribed to them by the sources or inherent in them is a control on whether these practices were

---

[1]A Cappella Music in the Public Worship of the Church (Abilene: Biblical Research Press, 1972), now in a revised third edition (Fort Worth: Star Bible Publications, 1999).

[2]"The Lord's Supper and Biblical Hermeneutics," Mission 10 (September, 1976):11-14; reprinted as "The Breaking of Bread," Gospel Advocate 133 (June, 1991):52-55.

incidental to the texts or were culturally and temporally conditioned. Is there a doctrinal meaning for the practice that determines its continuing relevance for the church? This criterion does not mean, "Can one attribute a doctrinal meaning to the practice?" (one can ascribe a doctrinal meaning to almost anything). The theology must derive from the texts and be intimately associated with the practice.

Unlike the other topics to which I have applied this methodolgy, the role of women in the assembly of the church is the subject of explicit New Testament prohibitions and commands. For that reason, the treatment of the New Testament texts must be much more extensive and the exegesis more detailed, even if not as exhaustive as a full scale commentary would require. The historical and doctrinal chapters will be briefer, for they are confirmatory of the exegesis and draw out its rationale and significance.

The material in Chapter 1 is based on and is an elaboration of material presented in my Inman Forum lectures for 1998 at Ohio Valley College and published for limited circulation under the title Some Contemporary Issues Concerning Worship and the Christian Assembly, Chapter 5, pp. 61-83. Part of the material in Chapter 2 is found in my Early Christians Speak, third edition (Abilene: ACU Press, 1999), pp. 225-237, and Early Christians Speak, Volume 2 (Abilene: ACU Press, 2002), pp. 267-279. Some of the doctrinal discussion in Chapter 3 comes out of these earlier treatments.[3]

_____

[3]For other writings expressing my viewpoint see the following: Everett Ferguson, The Church of Christ: A Biblical Ecclesiology for Today (Grand Rapids: Eerdmans, 1996), pp. 337-344; idem, Review of Carroll Osburn, Women in the Church, The Christian Chronicle (September, 2001), p. 32; Nancy Ferguson, "The Role of Women in the Assembly of the Church," in Jim Sheerer and Charles L. Williams, eds., Directions for the Road Ahead: Stability in Change among Churches of Christ (Chickasha, OK: Yeomen Press, 1998), pp. 41-53; Allan McNicol, "Scriptural Teaching on Women: Occasional Advice or Norm for the Ages?" Review of Carroll Osburn, Women in the Church, Christian Studies 18 (2000/2001), pp. 69-74.

1

NEW TESTAMENT TEXTS

Women's Activities in the Church

In addition to women's place in the home and family (leaving this topic aside for this study implies no depreciation of its importance), women were prominent in many activities in the early church. One of these was prophesying. Acts 2:17-18 claims the fulfillment of Joel 2:28-29, "Your sons and your daughters shall prophesy . . . . Even upon my slaves, both men and women, in those days I will pour out my Spirit; and they shall prophesy." Acts 21:9 mentions the four virgin daughters of Philip who had the gift of prophecy. First Corinthians 11:5 gives the regulation, "Any woman who prays or prophesies with her head unveiled disgraces her head." The setting in which this activity was done will be discussed later.

Along with prophesying, women were also engaged in teaching. Acts 18:26, "When Priscilla and Aquila heard him [Apollos], they took him aside and explained the Way of God to him more accurately." Titus 2:3-5 instructs, "Tell the older women to be reverent in behavior, not to be slanderers or slaves to drink; they are to teach what is good, so that they may encourage the young women."

Women worked in advancing the gospel. The details of this work are left unspecified, but the terminology is the same as used for men who were co-workers of the apostles and evangelists. Philippians 4:3 requests, "I ask you also, my loyal companion, help

7

these women [Euodia and Syntyche], for they have struggled beside me in the work of the gospel, together with Clement and the rest of my co-workers." This activity included missionary work. In Romans 16:7, Andronicus and Junia, who were "prominent among the apostles," were likely a husband and wife missionary team. The phrase does not mean "well known by the apostles" but "notable among the apostles," and Junia is almost certainly a feminine name.[4] "Apostles" is used in the sense of "missionaries" (as in Acts 14:4, 14; 2 Cor. 11:5, 13).

Women were also working on behalf of the church, again in unspecified ways. Romans 16:6, "Greet Mary, who has worked very hard among you." Romans 16:12, "Greet those workers in the Lord, Tryphaena and Tryphosa" (women's names).

Well-to-do women served by hosting the church in their homes. The wealthy Lydia provided the meeting place at the beginning of the church in Philippi, according to Acts 16:15 and 40: "When she and her household were baptized, she urged us, saying, 'If you have judged me to be faithful to the Lord, come and stay at my home.' . . . After leaving the prison, [Paul and Silas] went to Lydia's home; and when they had seen and encouraged the brothers and sisters there, they departed." The many benefactions of Phoebe (Rom. 16:2), of whom more below, may have included providing her home as a place of hospitality for missionaries and place of meeting for the church.

Women are mentioned as serving in various capacities that are specified. During Jesus' ministry women provided financial

---

[4]So the early church preacher and commentator John Chrysostom, Homilies on Romans 31 on Rom. 16:7 (trans. in Nicene and Post-Nicene Fathers, First Series, Vol. 11, p. 555).

support for him and the disciples. Luke 8:1-3, refers to women "who provided for them out of their resources." After the church began, Acts 9:36 refers to Dorcas, who "was devoted to good works and acts of charity," including making clothing for widows (vs. 39).

It is an open question whether women were recognized for their services to the church as female deacons. Romans 16:1-2 says of Phoebe, "I commend to you our sister Phoebe, a servant [diakonos, deacon] of the church at Cenchreae, . . . for she has been a benefactor of many and of myself as well." A benefactor or patron(ess) was a person with resources who provided for others and received duties from them in return. Since the predominant use of diakonos in the New Testament is as a general term and only seldom as a technical term for an appointed and representative servant of the church (as in Phil. 1:1 and 1 Tim. 3:8), it may be too much (although possible) to claim the latter meaning for Phoebe. First Timothy 3:11, on the other hand, has a better claim to refer to women deacons, but the meanings "wives" or (less likely) "women servants" cannot be ruled out. The position of deacon (=servant) was a serving role, and in the organizational structure of the church referred to assistants who functioned under the supervision of the bishops/elders.

There can be little doubt of another category in the church of women servants, who had qualifications, were appointed for specific duties, and received support from the church--the enrolled widows. First Timothy 5:3-16 identifies three kinds of worthy widows: those supported by their family (5:4, 8, 16), those supported by the charity of the church (5:3, 5, 16), and those who were enrolled by the church and engaged in ministries of service on its behalf (5:9-12).

Christians must confess that churches have not always utilized women as fully as these passages indicate they were involved in apostolic days. In reflecting cultural norms of the past the church through history has sometimes not only failed to put women to work fully but has even allowed their repression. Under the pressure of different cultural norms in the present, the church should not abandon scriptural standards concerning male and female roles. Both reactions are wrong. Cultural practices and societal preferences should not lead the church into either error, either placing undue restrictions on women's work or not respecting Biblical limitations. The cultural setting will certainly influence the extent to which women are involved and the ways in which that involvement is expressed, but in every cultural setting the church will respect both the dignity of women as made in the image of God and the divinely appointed leadership of men in the home and in the church (of which more in chapter 3). One must not defend the suppression of women in order to maintain Biblical teaching about male leadership in home and church.

Congregational Activities

Our immediate subject, however, is not these larger concerns of male-female relationships nor even women's general involvement in the life of the church. In two areas the New Testament places limitations on women's role: in one by the positive requirements about who can fill the function and in the other by the negative restrictions imposed. The requirements for a bishop/elder (1 Tim. 3:1-7; Titus 1:5-9) include the specification that this person be a married man with a family. More will be said about this in the doctrinal portion of this study. The second area where there is a limitation has to do with the assembly. Our concern now is with this latter topic. What specifically are women's roles in the congregational meeting of the church?

In the assembly women do the things commanded of each

Christian. These activities would include singing. Ephesians 5:18-20, "Do not get drunk with wine, for that is debauchery; but be filled with the Spirit, as you sing psalms and hymns and spiritual songs [to one another], singing and making melody to the Lord in your hearts, giving thanks to God the Father at all times and for everything in the name of our Lord Jesus Christ." These instructions apply to everyone (men are not the only ones to avoid drunkenness) and "at all times," so including the times of assembly. Women would join in the congregational "Amen" accompanying prayer (1 Cor. 14:16). Giving too is commanded of each Christian. 1 Corinthians 16:2, "On the first day of every week, *each of you* is to put aside and place in the treasury whatever is in keeping with your prosperity, so that collections need not be taken when I come."

The women, therefore, participate in the group activities of the congregation. The principle of joint participation expressed in these verses would cover unison scripture readings, unison prayer (e.g., reciting the "Lord's prayer" or other set prayer), unison confessions of faith, and other joint vocal expressions. What the whole congregation does together includes women. Individual activities must be evaluated separately. Individual activities are not the same as group participation. Leadership is not the same as joint congregational activity. What then about leadership roles in the assembly? To these we now turn, as we examine two passages that place limitations on women's activities in the assembly--1 Corinthians 14:33-40 and 1 Timothy 2:1-15.

Structure of 1 Corinthians 14:27-36

In order to interpret 1 Corinthians 14:33-40 correctly, one must place it in its immediate context. For this purpose the structural parallels of the instructions in verses 27-36 are helpful. The instructions to women are part of a series of regulations

11

concerning speaking in the assembly. Paul regulates the speech in turn of those who spoke in tongues (1 Cor. 14:27-28), the prophets (vss. 29-33), and women (vss. 33-36). Paul's regulations follow the same form in all three cases: name the group, state the rule about speech, give an example in conditional form, and justify what has been said.[5] I may set out the passage in chart form:

[Name the group]   If anyone <u>speaks</u> in a **tongue**
[State the rule about speech]   Let there be only two or at most three
                                                  and each in turn;
                                                  and let one interpret.
[An example in conditional form] But if there is no one to interpret,
                                                  <u>let them be silent in church</u>
[Justify the rule]   and <u>speak</u> to themselves and to
                                                  God.

[Name the group]   Let **prophets**
[State the rule about speech]   <u>speak</u> two or three,
                                                  and let the others [prophets?]
                                                  weigh what is said.
[An example in conditional form]   If a revelation is made to someone
                                                  else sitting nearby,
                                                  <u>let the first person be silent</u>.
                                                  You can all prophesy
                                                  one by one so that all
                                                  may learn and all be
                                                  encouraged.
[Justify the rule]   And the spirits of prophets are
                                                  subject to the prophets,
                                                  for God is a God not of disorder

---

[5]I am indebted here to Antoinette Clark Wire, "Prophecy and Women Prophets in Corinth," in James E. Goehring et al., <u>Gospel Origins and Christian Beginnings</u> (Sonoma: Polebridge, 1990), pp. 134-150.

	but of peace.
[Name the group	Let the **women**
[State the rule about speech]	be silent in the churches.
	For they are not permitted to speak,
	but should be subordinate, as the law also says.
[An example in conditional form]	If there is anything they desire to know, let them ask their husbands at home.
[Justify the rule]	For it is shameful for a woman to speak in church.

The chart shows three things: (1) All this passage is part of the same unit, so the words about women are not misplaced and are not an interpolation. (2) "Speak" and "Be silent" mean the same for women as for tongue speakers and prophets. (3) Paul is correcting disorders in the Corinthian assemblies. These include disruptive speech. The chart highlights the difference in dealing with the three groups: Paul regulates the speech of two groups and forbids that of the other group.

No known manuscript or other witness to the text lacks verses 34-35. A small group of closely related witnesses places them after verse 40. The most likely explanation for this displacement is that a scribe accidentally omitted the verses and added them when the omission was recognized. He did this either in the margin and the next scribe inserted them after verse 40 or he himself inserted them after verse 40. The argument for their unPauline character cannot be sustained.[6]

---

[6]E. Earle Ellis, The Making of the New Testament Documents (Leiden: Brill, 1999), pp. 426-434 argues that the indications that some

Another approach to 1 Corinthians 14:34-35 is to argue that it is Paul's quotation of a position taken by some of the Corinthians, which Paul peremptorily rejects in verse 36. However, when Paul in 1 Corinthians uses the conjunction "or" ($\bar{e}$), as in verse 36, he often is extending his argument or advancing a further consideration (e.g., 1 Cor. 1:13; 6:9, 19; 9:6, 7, 10; 10:22; 11:22; 12:21). When he rejects a quoted statement or slogan, he uses the strong adversative "but" (alla), as in 6:12 and 10:23

Limitations on Women's Speaking in the Assembly-- 1 Corinthians 14:33-40

The words "speaking" and "being silent" addressed to women are defined by their usage in the preceding verses (27-32). Some have tried to find a special meaning in the word for "speak" (laleō) in verse 34, for instance its association with tongue speaking in this chapter,[7] but the word is an ordinary word in Greek for any kind of speaking or other vocal sounds. It is used in this chapter also for the speaking by prophets (vss. 3 and 29) and by Paul for his intelligible speech (vs. 19). Similarly, the "silence" (sigaō) enjoined on women is the same silence enjoined on tongue speakers and prophets under the circumstances mentioned in this context. Being silent is the cessation or absence of speech. Without an indication otherwise, the words for speaking and being silent should have the same meaning as elsewhere in the context.

In the case of the tongue speakers and the prophets, Paul

---

interpreters find for an insertion result from Paul himself adding the words to a first draft of the letter

[7]Noted by Ralph P. Martin, The Spirit and the Congregation: Studies in 1 Corinthians 12-15 (Grand Rapids: Eerdmans, 1984), pp. 71 and 85.

regulates their speech and does not prohibit it altogether. He seeks to control abuses on the part of tongue speakers by limiting their number, making them take turns, and requiring the presence of an interpreter. Speaking in tongues was primarily speech addressed to God (1 Cor. 14:2, "For those who speak in a tongue do not speak to other people but to God"; cf. 13:1), not speech to the congregation. Paul had no problem with the private exercise of the gift (1 Cor. 14:2, 4-5 ["those who speak in a tongue build up themselves"], 18); this gift had a place in a congregational meeting, however, only if it was interpreted (1 Cor. 14:27-28), so that the others present could ratify the words addressed to God by saying "Amen" (1 Cor. 14:16). Prophets too were limited in number and were to speak in turns, yielding to someone else who had a revelation. Prophets brought the word of God to the people (1 Cor. 14:3-4, "Those who prophesy speak to other people for their upbuilding, encouragement, and consolation"; "those who prophesy build up the church"). Paul instructs tongue speakers when they may speak (one at a time) and when they should keep silent (absence of an interpreter); he instructs prophets when they may speak (one at a time) and when they should be silent (revelation made to another prophet).

In contrast to these regulations, Paul's prohibition on women speaking is stated absolutely; provision is made only for their silence, not their speaking. If Paul only wanted to regulate abuses, he could have done so and stated the circumstances under which women were to speak and the circumstances under which they were not. That is what he did in regard to tongue speakers and prophets.

It is sometimes argued that if one has a gift (e.g. a woman with a gift for teaching and speaking in public), she should be able to exercise it in the assembly. However, to have a gift did not guarantee the right to exercise it in church. Speaking in tongues was a gift inspired by the Holy Spirit (1 Cor. 12:10-11), but limitations were placed on its use in church and in some circumstances it was forbidden altogether (1 Cor. 14:18-19, 27-28).

The impersonal statement, "It is not permitted for them to speak" (vs. 34) indicates a general principle or law and not the statement of Paul's personal opinion or preference. The contrast ("But") stated in the imperative, "let them be in submission" or "let them subject themselves" (which would be better renderings than "subordinate"), shows that the speaking would indicate a lack of submission and so suggests that the speaking has to do with authoritative and representative public speaking roles.

The kinds of speaking under consideration in the context are that done by prophets (in bringing the word of the Lord to the assembly) and by tongue speakers (who speak to God--verse 2). That would be speaking done by a leader or a representative. Being silent is ceasing from those kinds of speech. Such would be, at a minimum, the kinds of speech excluded by the prohibition. In contemporary terms, the prohibition would exclude women from preaching (bringing the word of God to the people) and leading in prayer (speaking for the people to God) in the assembly. Since the speech of prophets included not only revelation (1 Cor. 14:6, 30) but also words of "edification, encouragement, and consolation" (1 Cor. 14:3), the prohibition on women's speech of that type would not be limited to "authoritative" teaching. The possibility, furthermore, must be allowed that since Paul gives separate attention to women speaking, he may be referring to some additional kind of speech beyond that of prophets and tongue speakers. In view of the variety of purposes served by prophetic speech, other kinds of messages than revelatory or authoritative speech may be included in what was forbidden to women.

Some have argued that the problem at Corinth was not

women prophesying but women prophets embarrassing their husbands by publicly questioning or examining (weighing, discerning--vs. 29) their prophetic speech in the assembly (hence, the stress on "their own husbands" in vs. 35).[8] In this case the questioning of verse 35 may have been the kind of examining or passing judgment on the prophetic utterances called for in verse 29. Or, the questioning of verse 35 may have been the use of questions as a teaching technique, as was done by Socrates and by the rabbis (and still employed). If so, this was not asking for information but taking an authoritative teaching role. There may be some validity to this as regards one of the specific circumstances that called forth Paul's regulations, but it is difficult to understand how questioning the prophetic utterance of her husband would assert more authority over him than delivering her own prophetic message. To restrict Paul's prohibition of women's speaking to this circumstance ignores the structure of the passage. The prohibition on women speaking is stated absolutely. If Paul only wanted to regulate abuses, he could have done so and stated the conditions under which women were to speak and the conditions under which they were not. That is what he did when there was only disorderly speech under consideration.

The example stated in the conditional clause, "If they wish to learn" (vs. 35), instead of being the type of speech that was creating a problem and so being forbidden, could be, on the pattern of the other conditional clauses in regard to tongue speakers and prophets, a special circumstance. On this alternative interpretation of the situation postulated in the conditional clause Paul extends the prohibition to the seemingly most innocent and justifiable kind of speaking, especially in view of Paul's own emphasis in the chapter

---

[8]E. Earle Ellis, Pauline Theology: Ministry and Society (Grand Rapids: Eerdmans, 1989), pp. 67-71.

on edification. The women might have argued that if you want us to be instructed, we ought to be able to ask questions so that we can learn what is meant. Paul's response is, if they do indeed want to learn, they have another venue in which to do so.

The Greek word for "husband" (anēr; plural andres) is also the word "male" or "man" and this broader meaning may be included here (1 Cor. 14:35). Even so, I take the "women" (gunaikes) of verse 34 (singular gunē, vs. 35) not to be limited to "wives." Unmarried women would hardly be given more freedom to address the assembly than married women. The objection that an unmarried woman had no one to ask does not apply here. Every woman in Greek society had a "man" as a legal representative. Her "man" here might be her husband, father, brother, or uncle.

We may never be able to establish with absolute persuasive-ness the occasion for disturbance that prompted Paul's regulations. All that we know for certain is what he laid down as the rules for conduct in the assembly. There is little room for doubt about what these rules are.

The passage advances four reasons for the silence of women in the assembly. (1) The first is the practice of the churches (1 Cor. 14:33, "As in all the churches of the saints"). The New Revised Standard Version and New International Version (as others) are probably correct in construing this clause with what follows in verse 34 rather than with what precedes in verse 33. Even in the latter case, the principle would apply to the whole passage. Paul often in 1 Corinthians underscores that his teaching to the Corinthians was what he delivered to all the churches (1 Cor. 4:17; 7:17; 11:16; 14:33). Thus he countered the tendency of the Corinthians to "go their own" and "do their own thing" (note his rebuke in 1 Cor. 14:36). The appeal to the practices of all the churches is an appeal to what had been delivered by apostles and evangelists to the churches and so to a common authoritative teaching. The practice was not something that varied with geographical location and so with local social customs.

(2) The second argument for the silence of women in church is based on the <u>law</u>. "They should be submissive, as the law also says" (1 Cor. 14:34). Such an appeal to what "the law says" is not uncharacteristic of Paul (cf. the same phrase in 1 Cor. 9:8). The "law" for Paul without some other qualification in the context normally means "the law of Moses" (so in 1 Cor. 9:9) or the Hebrew scriptures in general (1 Cor. 14:21 quotes from Isaiah as "the law"). In the case of 1 Corinthians 14:34, however, there is no explicit statement corresponding exactly to Paul's affirmation. "As the law says" is most often taken as referring to Genesis 3:16, which does refer to the husband's authority over his wife. Another possibility is suggested by 1 Corinthians 11:8-9, 12, where Paul bases subordination on creation according to Genesis 2:22, not on the fall. If these earlier words are still in mind, then Genesis 2 may be the basis of his statement. To whom the women are to be subject or subordinate, or better "be submissive," is not stated; where husbands are intended this is said (as in Eph. 5:22; Col. 3:18). This absence of an object generalizes the statement and argues against a limitation to husbands in this context. So too does the absence of the article with "woman" in the last part of verse 35; by omitting the article before "woman" Paul seems to be generalizing the prohibition. Even if the statements are not limited to wives and husbands, this submission, of course, is in the assembly, not a general command for women to be subordinate to men. Whether Paul has in mind Genesis 2:22, Genesis 3:16, or a deduction from the general tenor of the law, his reasoning is based on the law governing male-female relations (whether from creation or since the fall) and so has to do with the natural order, something that is not

subject to cultural changes. It is true that in Christ many things are renewed and therefore are different, but the distinctions of male and female are not canceled so far as life in this world is concerned (see more below on 1 Cor. 11). Part of Paul's problem with the Corinthians was their over-realized eschatology in which they thought of themselves as already living in the circumstances of the world to come (see 1 Cor. 4:8) and so were putting into practice ideals that do not belong to the present life.

(3) The third reason for women not to speak in church is that to do so is a matter of <u>shame</u>. Paul does not say that it is shameful to speak in a disorderly or disrespectful manner, as if that were the problem, but that "it is shameful for a woman to speak in church" (1 Cor. 14:35). The structure of the passage gives a central significance to this statement.[9] "Shame" ordinarily is culturally defined and was a major determinant of conduct in Mediterranean society, but here, given Paul's weighty declarations about the law and the command of God, it may be that the "shame" is defined by God and not by society. If Paul in this statement is thinking of what was culturally shameful, that still does not nullify his other reasons for his instructions.

(4) Paul climaxes his regulations with an appeal to the <u>command of the Lord</u>. "Anyone . . . must acknowledge that what I

---

[9]Terence Paige, "The Social Matrix of Women's Speech at Corinth: The Context and Meaning of the Command to Silence in 1 Corinthians 14:33b-36," <u>Bulletin for Biblical Research</u> 12 (2002):217-242, which contains a lot of good material but limits the meaning to a prohibition of ordinary conversation with men who were not relatives, which was shameful in Greek society. This makes the mistake many make of reconstructing the occasion for the prohibition and then limiting its application to the hypothetically reconstructed context.

am writing to you is a command of the Lord" (1 Cor. 14:37). This statement applies to the whole preceding discussion about disorders in the meetings at Corinth, but it certainly includes his words about women. No diminution can be made in regard to Paul's argument four. There is no cultural conditioning or relativity about a "command of the Lord."

These theological reasons may be contrasted with the arguments about the head covering for women in 1 Corinthians 11:2-6.

1 Corinthians 11:2-16

As I read 1 Corinthians 11:2,[10] I would reconstruct the literary situation somewhat like this. Through their letter or through personal communication the Corinthians have said that they observe the

---

[10]Among the many studies of the passage, note for valuable material, in spite of my disagreement on several points, L. Ann Jervis, "'But I Want You to Know . .' Paul's Midrashic Intertextual Response to the Corinthian Worshipers (1 Cor. 11:2-6)," Journal of Biblical Literature 112 (1993): 231-246 (good for the perspective on the problem and Paul's strategy for its correction); A. C. Perriman, "The Head of a Woman: The Meaning of kephale in I Cor. 11:3," Journal of Theological Studies, n.s. 45 (1994): 602-622 (man is woman's representative; the issue is whether the woman's behavior brings glory or dishonor on the man); J. D. BeDuhn, "'Because of the Angels': Unveiling Paul's Anthropology in 1 Cor. 11," Journal of Biblical Literature 118 (1999):295-320 (good exposition of the passage; angels responsible for creation of woman); Loren Stuckenbruck, "Why Should Women Cover Their Heads Because of the Angels? (1 Cor. 11:10)," Stone-Campbell Journal 4 (2001):205-234 (clothing a matter of sex distinction).

traditions Paul delivered to them. These include the custom of women wearing a head covering in public and men not. But in this matter, the Corinthians are wondering, "Why?" In Roman religion, both men and women in the act of offering sacrifice veiled their heads.[11] Moreover, the women in the church may have been pressing for full eschatological equality with men, so there is more attention to the question of women here. Even if women were accustomed to covering their head outside the home, they would not in the home, so if a group were meeting in one's home, the women of the house would have seen no reason to change their attire when other Christians were present.

In response to the Corinthians' comments or questions, Paul in 1 Corinthians 11 commends them for their observing his traditions but then goes on to offer reasons why in that cultural setting he made the distinction he did between male and female appearance in regard to a head covering. His subject here is the head covering and justification for it, not other matters.

The question may be asked, "If Christian women for the most part today ignore 1 Corinthians 11:2-16, why not also 14:34-35?"

---

[11]The usual translation "veil" may be misleading, for modern readers tend to think of Muslim women whose whole face except for the eyes is covered. The Greco-Roman "veil," as shown by sculpture and paintings, was the end of the garment pulled over the head, something like a shawl, leaving all the face visible. Richard Oster, "When Men Wore Veils to Worship: The Historical Context of 1 Corinthians 11:4," New Testament Studies 34 (1988):481-505; Cynthia Thompson, "Hairstyles, Head-coverings, and St. Paul: Portraits from Roman Corinth," Biblical Archaeologist 51 (1988):99-115; David W. J. Gill, "The Importance of Roman Portraiture for Head Coverings in 1 Cor. 11:2-16," Tyndale Bulletin 41 (1990):245-260.

The answer lies in the difference in the premises of the reasoning. Both passages are based on a ranking of male and female at creation. Male and female distinctions were instituted by God (1 Cor. 11:3, 8-9, 11-12; 14:34). Some of the ways in which those distinctions are observed are conditioned by societal norms; some are not.

According to 1 Corinthians 11:3 the divine order of leadership is God, Christ, man, woman. This was established at creation and is intended to promote mutuality. Woman was created second to man, was made from him, and made for him; but man now comes through woman, and the one is not independent of the other; and all things come from God (1 Cor. 11:8-9, 11-12). According to 1 Corinthians 11:8-9 Paul bases his instructions about women on Genesis 2, not Genesis 3. On these theological and anthropological premises Paul affirms that the distinction of the sexes is to be shown in their attire and appearance. The man should not have a head covering because he is the image and glory of God but the woman is the glory of man and her hair is a glory to her (1 Cor. 11:7, 15). Some of the specifics of how this gender distinction is applied depends on the cultural setting.

Notice how Paul's reasons for the head covering for women and its absence for men are loaded with the language of culture. (1) Honor or shame (disgrace) for the man--"any man who prays or prophesies with something on his head disgraces his head, but any woman who prays or prophesies with her head unveiled disgraces her head" (1 Cor. 11:4-5). (2) Shame (disgrace) to the woman--"It is one and the same thing as having her head shaved. . . . If it is disgraceful for a woman to have her hair cut off or to be shaved, she should wear a veil" (1 Cor. 11:5-6). (3) What is accepted as a sign of authority--"For this reason a woman ought to have a symbol of authority on her head" (1 Cor. 11:10). (4) What is regarded by human beings as <u>natural</u> (that is, what is customarily done)--"Judge for yourselves: is it proper for a woman to pray to God with her head unveiled? Does not nature itself teach you that if a man wears long hair, it is degrading to him, but if a woman has long hair, it is her glory?" (1 Cor. 11:13-15). (5) The <u>practice of the churches</u>--"We have no such custom, nor do the churches of God" (1 Cor. 11:16).

Honor and shame were major considerations in determining conduct in the societies of the ancient Mediterranean world. Several classical authors associate cutting off hair with shame for a woman, but this shame was not necessarily because of adultery or prostitution.[12] Since a culture tends to regard its customs as the "natural" way to do things, as the established order of things, "nature" (<u>physis</u>) had as one of its derived meanings "[accepted] custom."[13]

Observe that all of the considerations urged by Paul, with the possible exception of the fifth, refer to conditions or circumstances established by culture--having to do with honor, shame or disgrace, a sign or symbol, the natural or customary, and the customs of others. Where something is not considered a matter of honor or shame, has no symbolic significance, is not regarded as natural, then the specific expression has no force. These arguments are unlike the doctrinal affirmations in 14:34 and 37 about the law and

---

[12]Aristophanes, <u>Thesmophoriazusae</u> 836-838 (a woman who bore a wicked son should crop her hair in shame).; Tacitus, <u>Germania</u> 19 (Germans cut off the hair of an adulteress); Apuleius, <u>Metamporphoses</u> 7.6.3 (a woman cut off her hair and disguised herself like a man); Lucian, <u>Dialogi Meretricii</u> 5.3 (a prostitute who wore a wig removed it to appear to be a man)..

[13]John Chrysostom, <u>Homilies on 1 Corinthians</u> 37 takes the passage this way.

the command of the Lord. The distinction of male and female is an absolute and rests on creation; how that distinction is expressed is culturally relative.

Recognizing that 1 Corinthians 11 is discussing male-female roles as expressed in appearance may help to account for the apparent contradiction that many have observed between 1 Corinthians 11:2-16 and 1 Corinthians 14:33-35. 1 Corinthians 11:5 refers to a "woman who prays or prophesies" and 1 Corinthians 14:34-35, after discussing the exercise of the prayer language of tongues and the act of delivering prophecies, forbids a woman to speak in the assembly. And it may be that the Corinthian women were speaking publicly in these ways in the assembly; that would be why Paul had to speak so explicitly to the matter in 1 Corinthians 14. Yet, readers often wonder why Paul does not say anything negative about the practice at its first mention in 1 Corinthians 11 if he indeed thought the practice was wrong.

There is a current tendency to take 1 Corinthians 11:5 as normative practice in Pauline churches and find some narrower interpretation of 1 Corinthians 14:34-35. That seems to me to be a strange exegetical approach. Whereas, the subject in the early part of 1 Corinthians 11 is the head covering, and the speaking roles of praying and prophesying are incidental to the main subject, the subject in 1 Corinthians 14 is precisely speaking roles in the assembly and under what circumstances they are to be exercised. The instructions given in the primary discussion of the topic should be regulative.

One approach to the apparent contradiction is to postulate two different settings for 1 Corinthians 11 and 1 Corinthians 14. That 1 Corinthians 11:5 refers to an assembly of the church, comparable to that in 1 Corinthians 14:34-35, is widely assumed but seldom is a case made for the identification. When such is attempted the case rests on 1 Corinthians 11 being a public occasion, since men and women are presumably present and to prophesy was an act in the worship assembly,[14] and the presumed connection of verses 2-16 with verses 17-34. Both arguments are open to question. The options are not limited to what is private and what is done in the church assembly. Something could be public and not be a meeting of the church. The assembly was not the only place where prophecy was delivered. Acts 21:8-12 describes a prophet speaking to a group that is not an assembly of the church. The group addressed by Agabus included Paul, his traveling companions (seven are named in 20:4, to whom Luke is to be added on the basis of the "we"), and perhaps also Philip and his four virgin daughters (who also had the gift of prophecy), since their home was where Paul's company was staying. Yet this was not a "church," not an assembly of the church even though all present were Christians. As to the connection of 1 Corinthians 11:2-16 with 17-34, the words of verse 17, contrasted with verse 2, could be understood as taking up a different setting as well as a different topic. There could be public occasions of prayer and prophecy where women were the spokespersons but not be the times when "the whole church comes together" envisioned in 1 Corinthians 14 (note vs. 23). That distinction removes any contradiction between 1 Corinthians 11 and 14. On this explanation there were occasions that were not an assembly of the whole church when women prayed and prophesied in public.

Another approach to reconciling 1 Corinthians 11:5 and 14:34-35 is to grant that 11:5 may be an assembly but conclude that

---

[14]Gordon D. Fee, The First Epistle to the Corinthians, The New International Commentary on the New Testament (Grand Rapids: Eerdmans, 1987), p. 505.

Paul addresses one problem at a time: the head covering in chapter 11 and women speaking in chapter 14. Although this approach is often scoffed at, it closely parallels what Paul did in dealing with meat sacrificed to idols in 1 Corinthians 8-10. His strategy there was to accept the premises of the Corinthians who were arguing for their freedom to eat such meat but to contest on other grounds (the effects on others) their conclusion about the practice (8:1-13), and then to turn to detailed regulations of the circumstances in which sacrificial meat may be eaten and not eaten (10:14-33). Indeed many mistakenly assume on the basis of 1 Corinthians 8 that for Paul eating sacrificial mean was theologically indifferent,[15] even as many conclude from 1 Corinthians 11:5 that Paul approved of women prophesying in church. In both cases there is a failure to give full weight to his detailed regulations that come later.

Failure to observe Paul's pattern of argument could lead to the conclusion that there is a contradiction between 1 Corinthians 8:4,7 and 10:14, 20-21, even as some conclude that there is a contradiction between 11:5 and 14:34-35. Paul's strategy in dealing with idol meat was first to agree with the principle advocated by some among the Corinthians (perhaps learned from him or misinterpreting something he taught). His limitation of its application or correction of it in practice is expressed with enough intervening material that the result appears to be a contradiction rather than a qualification. In 1 Corinthians 8:4-6 Paul agrees that "no idol in the world really exists" and "there is no God but one," and argues against "eating in the temple of an idol" (8:10) only on the basis of the effect on a weaker brother who does not have this knowledge (note 8:13 for Paul's strongly held position). But then in 1

---

[15]Alex T. Cheung, Idol Food in Corinth: Jewish Background and Pauline Legacy (Sheffield: Sheffield Academic Press, 1999), pp. 82-164 has the correct approach, even if he is not persuasive on every point.

Corinthians 10, when he comes to lay down regulations in regard to various situations, he says in verses 20-21 that "Pagans sacrifice to demons and not to God" and "You cannot partake of the table of the Lord and the table of demons." There was no contradiction in Paul's mind, for idols had no real existence, but the demons that stood behind idolatry were real and were to be avoided. Even on the partial truth of the premises of the Corinthians' argument there was reason to stay away from pagan temples. But Paul does not stop when he mentions the claim that idols do not exist to explain that there is more to the reality than this simple denial. He waits until he gets around to prescribing under what conditions meat sacrificed to an idol may or may not be eaten to declare the reality of demons. Since they are real, to eat in a temple meat sacrificed to an idol is forbidden.

It may be that Paul is doing something similar in 1 Corinthians 11 and 14. The discussion of reasons for a woman having a head covering and a man not having one is prompted by a request from the Corinthians for an explanation. The further ramifications involved in a woman's speaking in the assembly are reserved for the detailed regulations given later. To cite 1 Corinthians 11:5 as evidence for women praying and prophesying in church with Paul's approval (in disregard to 14:34-35) is to make the same mistake as to take 1 Corinthians 8:4-6, 10 as meaning that since idols are nothing it is all right for Christians to eat in their temples the meat sacrificed to them (in disregard of 10:20-21).

Although there is the widespread assumption that Paul in 1 Corinthians 11:5 "approves" of women prophesying and praying in public provided they wear a head covering, this text is descriptive, neither prescriptive nor approving.[16] Those who think 1 Corinthians 11:5 authorizes speaking roles for women should observe the condition it imposes--a head covering or a comparable cultural expression of submission (however, many of those who want women speaking in the assemblies don't like the idea of submission). If 1 Corinthians 11:5 authorizes women preaching and praying, why does it not authorize a veil, the clearly prescriptive part of the passage? Can those who take 1 Corinthians 11:5 as normative make the argument I made above about the culturally conditioned nature of the passage, which would include the "praying and prophesying" as well as the head covering? If speech inspired by the Holy Spirit--prophesy and (as argued above) prayer in the form of tongues--was subject to limitations, how much more would uninspired speech be?

Limitations on Women's Activities in the Assembly--- 1 Timothy 2:1-15

The other passage in addition to 1 Corinthians 14:34-36 that places limitations on women's activities in church is 1 Timothy 2:1-15.[17] The setting of 1 Corinthians 14 is clearly the assembly, for this is stated explicitly (vss. 19, 23, 34, 35). This setting is not so obvious in 1 Timothy 2; nevertheless, I find the evidence for this

---

[16]Assuming that the Corinthians were practicing a vicarious baptism for the dead, does one conclude that Paul's reference to the practice in 1 Cor. 15:29 approves or authorizes it?

[17]Without endorsing everything, I commend on 1 Timothy 2 the commentary by William D. Mounce, Pastoral Epistles (Word Bible Commentary; Nashville: Thomas Nelson, 2000).

interpretation persuasive.

The "instructions" (1 Tim. 1:18) given to Timothy have the character of a "church order," in which regulations are given about assembly, ministers and their appointment, discipline, and other matters affecting church life.[18] Paul indicates in 1 Timothy 3:15 that his regulations are for conduct "in church." On the pattern of a church order, the treatment of the assembly comes in 1 Timothy 2 and the qualifications of bishops and deacons in chapter 3. The formal description of types of prayers in 1 Timothy 2:1 and the specification that these prayers are for "every one" and especially for rulers (vs. 2) so that "we" (Christians, the church) might be at peace suggests a public, more formal gathering. In this context "men" (plural) pray, "lifting up holy hands" (a posture for public, although not exclusively so, prayer). The women are not to dress ostentatiously (vss. 9-10), that is for show in public (this would again not be exclusively applicable to the assembly, but fits that situation). The women are to learn in quietness with full submission and not to teach (vss. 11-12). These words about women learning but not teaching are hardly applicable to home and private settings (Titus 2:3-5). The conclusive point to my mind is the phrase "in every place" (1 Tim. 2:8). Although it is often taken to mean "everywhere," there is another Greek word that means "everywhere" (pantachou), and this phrase "in every place" often appears in Jewish and Christian usage with an almost technical meaning of "in every place of meeting" (1 Cor. 1:2; 2 Cor. 2:14; 1 Thess. 1:8).[19] This phrase

---

[18]Among such documents in the early church are the Didache, the Apostolic Tradition attributed to Hippolytus of Rome, and the Syriac Didascalia.

[19]Everett Ferguson, "Topos in 1 Timothy 2:8," Restoration Quarterly 33 (1991):65-73.

would be equivalent to the phrase "in church," or "in assembly" in 1 Corinthians 14.

Two activities are specified in 1 Timothy 2 as exercised by men--praying (that is, leading in prayer, expressly mentioned) and teaching (tacitly implied). These activities are denied to women, the one (leading in prayer) tacitly and the other (teaching) expressly.

Verse 8, "I desire the men to pray," does not employ the generic "men," meaning "human beings," but the specific word for "males." This usage shows that only men are expected to provide leadership in prayer. Lifting hands in prayer is assumed (it was the common posture of prayer among Greeks, Romans, Jews [Ps. 28:2; 134:2], and Christians): the command is that the men are to pray with "holy" hands backed up by a conduct that is without anger and disputing. The phrase about "without anger or argument" perhaps indicates strife or contention in the congregation, but if so, such a situation would not limit the command for the prayer to be from a holy life free of anger and argumentativeness to the circumstance that called forth the command.

The instructions for women have to do first of all with their dress (1 Tim. 2:9-10). Some have tried to construe their appearance as parallel to men's lifting holy hands, so that Paul is interpreted as saying, "I wish the men to pray lifting holy hands and in the same manner the women to pray clothed with good works." But the statement about women's attire does not refer to the manner in which they lead in prayer; it is actually set off in contrast to the function of the men. Paul's "I wish" is completed by two infinitives, one referring to the men, "to pray" in a certain manner, and the other referring "likewise" to the women, "to adorn" or "to dress" themselves in a certain manner. Women's clothing is to be associated with good works and an expression of godliness. The basic principle of modest dress is timeless; women at no time are to "show off" with "gold, pearls, or expensive clothes." Hair braided with gold was a cultural expression at the time of writing that was an example of immodest dress. Simple braided hair in my youth was an expression of a very plain appearance, but statuary from the later first century shows examples of elaborate coiffures worn by noble ladies that are the very different kind of braided hair forbidden here.

In contrast to the men's role of leading in prayer, the women are forbidden "to teach or to have authority over a man" (1 Tim. 2:12). Some take the two items forbidden to be only one, that is teaching in an authoritative, domineering, or assertive manner. However, most examples of the construction "not [ouk] . . . nor [oude]" ("not to teach nor to have authority") in the New Testament link parallel statements, so that two items are negated.[20] If the second word or phrase qualifies the first in some way, the second explains the significance or meaning of the first (as in Rom. 2:28, "not a Jew outwardly, nor is circumcision outward and physical"; Matt. 6:20, "not break in nor steal"; 1 Thess. 5:5, "not of night nor darkness"). According to this usage, for a woman to teach a man is for her to exercise authority over or domineer him. A similar construction to 1 Timothy 2:12 occurs in 6:16, "No one [oudeis] has ever seen God, nor can see him." In this case the second statement carries the thought further or gives the basis for it. On this parallel 2:12 would mean that the woman is forbidden to teach and certainly not take an authoritative position over the man. The full construction in 1 Timothy 2:12 is ouk . . . oude . . . alla (not to teach, nor domineer, but to be in quietness). In such a construction both of the first two items are negated and the following positive statement carries the weight of the meaning. Galatians 1:1 is an

---

[20]Frederick William Danker, A Greek-English Lexicon of the New Testament and Other Early Christian Literature, third edition (Chicago: University of Chicago Press, 2000), p. 734.

example--Paul's apostleship came neither from a human being nor through a human being but through Christ and God. According to this parallel the command in 1 Timothy 2:12 is for women not be in positions of teaching or domination of a man but to be quiet learners. The normal use of the grammatical construction in 1 Timothy 2:12 argues against an application of the prohibition to only one type of teaching.

Women are to "learn" (1 Tim. 2:11), not "teach" (1 Tim. 2:12). Instead of the passage reflecting a cultural norm, the provision for the woman to learn actually contrasts with a strand of Jewish thought reflected in rabbinic literature. The Palestinian Talmud includes the quotation: "Better to burn the Torah than to teach it to a woman" (ySotah 3.19a,3, but see further in chapter 2 below).

It is twice stated that the women are to be "in quietness" (1 Tim. 2:11-12). This word (hēsuchia) refers to a state of quietness without disturbance but, although a different word from "silence" in 1 Corinthians 14, can have that meaning in some contexts (cf. Acts 22:2; and one manuscript of 21:40 instead of sige) and is rendered "silence" in the NRSV of 1 Timothy 2:11-12. The learning is to be not only in quietness but also in "all submission" (vs. 11). To whom the submission is given is not stated--to the persons teaching? Objects are not stated because the emphasis is on the woman's attitude, not on to whom submission is to be given.

The argument in 1 Timothy 2 has been limited by some interpreters to wives on the basis of similarities to the language employed for husband-wife relations in the household codes of the New Testament (1 Pet. 3:1-7; Eph. 5:21-33).[21] I would find the

---

[21]E. Earle Ellis, Pauline Theology: Ministry and Society (Grand Rapids: Eerdmans, 1989), pp. 71-78, a similar argument to what he employed on

similarities in content greater to church order type of material. Instructions from the household codes occur later in 1 Timothy, as on different age groups and slaves in 1 Timothy 5:1-2; 6:1-2 (cf. Titus 2:1-10; 3:1-2). Similarities in language are due to the parallel drawn in Timothy between the household and the church, a subject discussed in chapter 3 on doctrinal considerations. There would seem to be no reason why wives would be forbidden roles of praying and teaching that were permitted to single women. How would praying and teaching be an exercise of authority over her husband in a way that the same activities by a single woman were not? Where submission by wives to husbands is commanded, this is stated by naming them as the object to whom submission is due (Eph. 5:22; Col. 3:18) and is not left unexpressed, as is the case in 1 Timothy 2:11. Moreover, In verses 9, 11, 12 "woman" (gune) without an article is a generic noun. In verse 12, andros is again a generic singular. This usage is appropriate to a general rule and as in 1 Corinthians 14 argues against the meaning "wife," which normally would have the article.

The instructions in 1 Timothy 2 closely parallel those given in 1 Corinthians 14. Both prohibit women from praying and preaching or teaching in the church's assembly. As argued above, the prohibition of women teaching and exercising authority in 1 Timothy 2 applies to the assembly, as is the case in 1 Corinthians 14. Women may teach elsewhere. As noted in the beginning of this chapter, older women are commanded to teach younger women (Titus 2:3-5). And women taught men, privately and at home, as Priscilla did Apollos (Acts 18:26). The prohibition of exercising authority over men, therefore, is not a general principle applicable to any situation, but has a specific reference to the assembled church. These instructions then prepare the way for 1 Timothy 3, which gives

---

1 Corinthians 14:33-40.

the place of a bishop to a married man with a family.

Verses 13-14 of 1 Timothy 2 introduce the reasons for the limitations in verses 11-12. The conjunction "for" (gar) has been interpreted as supplying illustrations, but this usage is rare, and the word should be given its normal significance of supplying a cause or reason. The basis is the man's priority in creation (1 Tim. 2:13), as in 1 Corinthians 11:8-9. To this explanation is added the consideration of the woman's priority in the fall (1 Tim. 2:14). There is no necessary implication that women are more gullible or more susceptible to sin than men: Paul elsewhere makes Adam primarily responsible in the sin, another indication of the man's leadership and the responsibility that goes with it (Rom. 5:14; 1 Cor. 15:22, 45). Adam was first in creation; Eve was first in transgression. The two reasons are drawn from Genesis--verse 13 is based on Genesis 2:21-23, and verse 14 on Genesis 3:13. These theological reasons will be further developed in chapter 3.

Women have a function that men do not have, the bearing of children (1 Tim. 2:15); and men have a function of leadership in church based on the created order. The universal offer of salvation in verses 1-7 is applied in 1 Timothy 2:15 to women, specifically Eve. Perhaps the opponents were saying that for women to be saved they must give up conventional female roles (as some second-century ascetics advocated). "She [singular] will be saved" may refer to Eve (?) as representative of the women in Ephesus (hence the change to the plural in the phrase "if they continue"). "Salvation" normally means in the New Testament and in the Pastoral Epistles spiritual salvation from sins. Salvation is through accepting one's (in this case woman's) God-given role, if accompanied by faith, etc. "Modesty" is picked up from verse 9. The childbearing refers to a capacity, not a requirement; not every woman in fact has children. Neither does every man lead in prayer or teach in the church. A general principle is being stated here. As there is a function peculiar to women, so it seems there is a function reserved for men alone.

The unique female function of childbearing is obvious and is a matter of nature. Men's leadership in church is not something determined biologically, but 1 Timothy does seem to indicate that the instructions, which may appear to be arbitrary, are somehow founded on a distinction that goes back to creation and the natural order instituted by God. Moreover, as a consequence of the fall into sin, certain relationships between men and women have been imposed. This of course does not mean that women do not have the capacity to fill the public leadership role in the church; they may do it as well or better than men. That is not the question. As there is a function reserved for women, so there is a function that God for some reason has chosen to reserve for men. Salvation comes from respecting these distinct female and male roles.

These instructions in 1 Timothy 2 are universal in regards to the church, as everything about them indicates: prayer for all people (vs. 1), every place [of meeting] (vs. 8), women's attire (vss. 9-10), the formulation of a general rule (vss. 11-12), the appeal to origins (vss. 13-14), childbearing as a characteristic of women (vs. 15). To particularize part of the passage or limit it to a special problem in Ephesus is to ignore the whole tenor of the passage. That Paul gives essentially the same instructions to Corinth and to Ephesus shows that a common practice undergirded by a common theology is being presented.

Passages Used to Support Women Preaching

Various passages are cited by those who respect the authority of the Bible yet advocate the right of women to speak in the assembly. Among these are 1 Corinthians 11:5, discussed above, and Galatians 3:28, to be discussed in chapter 3. Some others will be noted here.

Joel 2:28-29 says, "Then afterward I will pour out my spirit on all flesh; your sons and your daughters shall prophesy, your old men shall dream dreams, and your young men shall see visions. Even on the male and female slaves, in those days, I will pour out my spirit." Peter expressly quotes these words as fulfilled in Acts 2:17. There were women prophetesses in Old Testament times (as Huldah, 2 Kings 22:14) and women judges (as Deborah, also called a prophetess, Judges 4:4), but no women priestesses. Similarly, there are women specified as having the gift of prophecy in the New Testament (as the four daughters of Philip, Acts 21:9), but no women elders. We are not given information about the setting in which these New Testament prophetesses delivered their message, but there is no certain indication that it was in the assemblies of the church (if 1 Cor. 11:5 indicates women were prophesying in church in Corinth, Paul prohibits the practice in 14:34).

I have read of Luke 11:27 being appealed to. Here a woman calls out in the crowd to Jesus, "Blessed is the womb that bore you and the breasts that nursed you!" This public testimony to Jesus occurred before the church came into existence and so is irrelevant to activities in the assembly. Women may still give public testimony to Jesus in other settings. And, note Jesus' response to her words, "Blessed rather are those who hear the word of God and obey it!" (Luke 11:28).

Similarly, the example of the Samaritan woman occurred during the personal ministry of Jesus before there was a church. She went back to her city and said to the people, "Come and see a man who told me everything I have ever done! He cannot be the Messiah, can he?" (John 4:29). "Many Samaritans from that city believed in Jesus because of the woman's testimony" (John 4:39). She was doing part of the work of an evangelist: telling her neighbors and friends about Jesus. Nothing precludes a woman doing today what she did; indeed we could wish we had more women, and men, doing this. There is an evangelism to be done outside the assembly in which women should be fully involved, as was Priscilla in Acts 18:26. But this activity has nothing to do with preaching in church.

Mistaken Strategies in Interpretation

Those respectful of Biblical authority who advocate women taking a public leadership role in the church employ various hermeneutical strategies in order to relativize the Biblical injunctions. One strategy is to limit the apostolic directions to the circumstances that gave rise to the correction.

A typical procedure, when neither the text under consideration nor another source makes explicit what the problem was, is to use clues in the text to reconstruct the situation addressed in the text (in this case 1 Cor. 14 and 1 Tim. 2). This procedure is quite proper to an extent and often the only way to proceed in trying to get a deeper and more accurate understanding of the text. The next step that is taken, however, is problematical, for it goes beyond exegesis to hermeneutics. This step is to limit the instructions to the reconstructed situation, making them local and cultural. Hence, the conclusion is drawn that the instructions in the passages apply to the present day only to the extent the situation is the same. This is an approach not allowed on other passages. For example, take the teaching on the Lord's supper in 1 Corinthians 11:17-34. Does a church have to have the same problems of division in the congregation (11:18) and selfish disregard of the poor (11:21-22) for the instructions about proper participation in the bread and fruit of

38

the vine (11:23-32) to be normative today?

The determination of the problem being addressed or the situation calling forth the instructions may or may not be correct; the more accurately we can reconstruct the situation the more exact we can make our interpretation. The mistake comes in moving from the exegesis to the hermeneutical application. To limit the instructions given in a particular historical situation to that situation is an interpretive judgment and does not derive from the text (unless the text itself makes that limitation). One's judgment about the application of a text is not the same as a "word of the Lord." Nearly all the Bible was addressed to specific historical situations. God spoke through his representatives in those situations in order to reveal truths and teaching applicable at other places and times. Paul, for example, spoke not simply to correct given situations; in making his corrections he not only employed practical arguments directed to the particular viewpoints of the recipients of his correspondence but he also spoke out of fundamental doctrinal positions. We should apply the principles and the instructions revealed in given historical circumstances to our own situation today. The text itself is our authority, not our reconstruction of the context.

Another strategy is to identify what one perceives to be the trend or the goal of Biblical revelation and then to regulate one's interpretation by that principle. On this approach one takes what seems to be the direction toward which Biblical teaching was leading and then concluding that what promotes this goal has Biblical authority. For instance, the Bible is seen to be on the side of liberty (as God freeing Israel from bondage in Egypt and Jesus bringing freedom from the guilt of sin) so that liberation (and that may be economic, social, or psychological as well as religious) becomes the key to interpreting how the Bible is to be applied to present-day situations. In regard to the subject of this booklet, the fundamental

Biblical teaching about male and female is identified as egalitarianism, and that principle is then made normative for the interpretation of texts.

The fallacy and subjectivity of this strategy of trying to discern the goal of Biblical revelation may be seen if the same approach is taken in the interests of female subordination (which is different from Biblical submission[22]). If subordination is seen as the prevailing tenor of Biblical teachings, then other passages may be interpreted in terms of this overruling principle. One may derive one's normative principle from scripture (equality on the one hand from Gen. 1:26-27; Gal. 3:28, or subordination on the other hand from 1 Cor. 14:34; 1 Pet. 3:7), but the principle is then absolutized so that everything else is either interpreted in terms of the chosen principle or ignored as temporary or irrelevant. This approach leaves our theology or our interpretation as the authority, not the words of scripture. Certainly, it is appropriate to try to determine the great Biblical doctrines and give central importance to them in interpreting Scripture, but the Biblical texts themselves must continue to guide us in doing so.

These mistaken strategies in interpretation have to do with the contemporary application of Biblical texts and so illustrate the difference between exegesis and hermeneutics. Exegesis has to do with determining the meaning of a text in its literary and historical context. The literary, grammatical, and lexical meanings of certain key texts have been the primary concern of this chapter. The historical context will be the concern of the next chapter. There is not much disagreement about what the Biblical and historical texts we are examining meant; disagreements in their exegesis have to do mainly with reconstructing the situations being addressed. The

---

[22]See Nancy Ferguson, Living a Worthy Life (Nashville: Gospel Advocate, 1999), pp. 165-192.

major problems have to do with the separate task of hermeneutics, namely the interpretation and application of a text in relation to the present-day. Theology is necessarily involved in hermeneutics and will be the concern in chapter 3.

2

EVIDENCE FROM HISTORY

The procedure in this chapter will be to sketch briefly information about women in the principal societies in which the church began and then to assemble some of the relevant texts from early church history in order to show what writings from outside the New Testament tell us about the practice of the earliest churches. It will be seen that the cultural context of the New Testament in regard to what was acceptable for women was not uniform and so offers no simple explanation for why the New Testament placed limitations on women's place in the churches. The church history evidence, in turn, is not authoritative for Christian practice today, but it shows a remarkable consistency with what has been learned from the exegesis of New Testament texts above: in the mainstream of the church women were very active in many ways but did not take public speaking roles nor did they fill the office of elder/bishop; only in those groups rejected by the main body of believers did women take these positions, and in doing so they may have been continuing the practices that 1 Corinthians 14 and 1 Timothy 2 sought to correct. The involvement of women in leadership positions in heretical and schismatic groups shows that the mainstream or orthodox churches could have done the same if they thought apostolic instructions permitted such.

Women in New Testament Backgrounds

No simple generalizations can be made about what was culturally acceptable or unacceptable for women in different places or in different times in the Greco-Roman world.[23] Moreover, in all societies of the first century wealth and social position gave some women an influence beyond what law and cultural norms would have dictated.

In classical Greece women were largely secluded, but they exercised greater independence in Hellenistic times. Their sphere was management of the household under the supervision of the husband. The conservative Greek view was still expressed by Plutarch in the early second century: "For a woman ought to do her talking either to her husband or through her husband, and she should not feel aggrieved if, like the pipe-player, she makes a more impressive sound through a tongue not her own" (Plutarch, Advice to Bride and Groom 32 [=Moralia 142D]). But Plutarch was not the whole story, and we have a wide range of views expressed and evidence of a great variety of activities in which women engaged, including the holding of civic offices. In Hellenistic religions women had more prominence and leadership than in other areas of life--serving as priestesses, being benefactors, and holding offices in cultic associations. A notable instance is the oracle at Delphi, not too far from Corinth, where the revelations of Apollo were always delivered through the mouth of a priestess (the Pythia).

Roman women had more public visibility and higher status than Athenian women. The legal view was that they were subject to a male: father, husband, or guardian. In the early empire, however,

---

[23]Excellent compilations of material may be found in Gregory E. Sterling, "Women in the Hellenistic and Roman Worlds (323 BCE--138 CE)," and Randall D Chesnutt, "Jewish Women in the Greco-Roman Era," in Carroll D. Osburn, ed., Essays on Women in Earliest Christianity, Vol. 1 (Joplin: College Presss, 1993), pp. 41-92, 93-130. For summary characteriztions and extensive bibliography see my Backgrounds of Early Christianity, 3rd ed. (Grand Rapids: Eerdmans, 2003).

they came to have greater freedom of action. Particularly notable is the prominence of priestesses in the civic cults[24] and their leadership in some of the mystery religions and other private religious associations.

Jewish women were not as restricted in public appearance as in classical Greece but did not have the freedom of first-century Roman women. The Jewish woman was mistress of the home, but she could not serve as a witness in court, normally could not initiate a divorce, and was exempt from most religious duties because of her monthly impurity. Rabbinic literature comes from a later period than the New Testament, but it reflects one strand in Judaism and is useful for comparison. Rabbis affirmed that women were equal to men before God, but women did not take a lead in synagogue services. They were present, and some rabbis said women and minors could read scripture, but the Sages said women should not do so (bMeg. 23a; tMeg. 3.11; 4.11). Some rabbis objected to women studying Torah (Sotah 3.4), but this probably referred to the oral law, for women were expected to listen to the scriptures in the synagogue (bHag. 3a). Jewish inscriptions refer to women as "head of the synagogue" (archisunagogos), "mother of the synagogue," "priestess," "elder," or "ruler" of the synagogue.[25] In some cases (like priestess) the title was given because of family connections (from a priestly family or given a title because of the husband's

---

[24]The evidence for nine priestesses in the official state cults in Pompeii in the first century, an example from only one city, is collected by Roy Bowen Ward, "The Public Priestesses of Pompeii," in Abraham J. Malherbe, et al., eds., The Early Church in Its Context: Essays in Honor of Everett Ferguson (Leiden: Brill, 1998), pp. 318-334.

[25]The evidence is collected and given a maximalist interpretation by Bernadette J. Brooten, Women Leaders in the Ancient Synagogue (Chico: Scholars Press, 1982)

position); in some cases the titles are honorary because the women were benefactors (like "mother of the synagogue"); but in some cases the titles were perhaps functional.

We cannot simply dismiss New Testament limitations on women as due to their place in society. That a given passage gives its instructions on the basis of what was culturally acceptable must be demonstrated in each case (as is attempted on 1 Corinthians 11:2-16 in chapter 1 above) and not simply asserted because of generalizations about first-century society.

Roles of Women According to Early Christian Literature

Were 1 Corinthians 14 and 1 Timothy 2 local and specific in their application? Or were they general and universal? One way to answer the question is by looking at the evidence from early church history for the general practice of the churches. Of course, the giving of essentially the same teaching to two different cities some two decades apart would indicate a general rule. Paul himself says his teachings were for all the churches--1 Corinthians 14:33. Church history indicates how the churches understood the apostolic teaching and practices. Those early churches could have been wrong, but their evidence should be considered. And that evidence becomes particularly strong when it is quite uniform and is corroborative of indications in the New Testament itself.

Mention is made in early Christian literature of women in various capacities.[26] Instructions are given for women as wives and

---

[26]See my Early Christians Speak, 3rd edition (Abilene: ACU Press, 1999), pp. 225-237, and Volume 2 (Abilene: ACU Press, 2002), pp. 267-279 for

mothers, similar to household codes of the New Testament (1 Clement 1.3; Polycarp, Philippians 4.2-3). Women were prominent among the martyrs (Eusebius, Church History 5.1.18-19, 41-42, 55-56 about Blandina; Passion of Perpetua and Felicitas; and others). They were notable in the practice of asceticism, and virgins were a recognized class in local churches before the rise of monasticism (Ignatius, Smyrnaeans 13; Polycarp, Philippians 5.3; Hippolytus [?], Apostolic Tradition 12). Women were missionaries, an example being Thecla (Acts of Paul and Thecla 41, 43). The circumstances in which Thecla "enlightened many with the word of God" are not detailed, but where information is given her teaching was to women in the household (Acts of Paul and Thecla 39). Clement of Alexandria refers to the wives of apostles evangelizing in the women's quarters of houses (Miscellanies 3.6.53).

Women had teaching functions outside the assembly. An early example is provided by the Shepherd of Hermas, where a woman exhorts women and children but men address the church. A female figure personifying the church gave Hermas the following instructions in a vision: "You shall write two little books and send one to Clement and one to Grapte [a woman's name]. Clement shall send it to the cities abroad...and Grapte shall admonish the widows and orphans. But you shall read it yourself in this city with the elders who preside over the church" (Visions 2.4.3).

What then about special appointed ministries?

Women with Special Ministries in the Church

Certain widows were appointed to a place of special service

---

translations and commentary on the texts.

in the church. The Apostolic Tradition attributed to Hippolytus (about A.D. 215) says that "when a widow is appointed, she is not ordained but she shall be chosen by name" (10.1). The passage continues by explaining that ordination (involving the laying on of hands) is for those that offer the eucharist or have a ministry in the liturgy. The enrolled widow "is appointed for prayer, and this is a function of all (Christians)" (10.5). The Didascalia (third century) provides for the appointment of widows to engage in prayer, benevolence, and care of the sick but not to teach. The Apostolic Church Order (about A.D. 300) chapter 5 distinguished two types of widows: one for prayer and the other for service to women in illness or need.

How early and how widespread the office of women deacons appeared depends on the interpretation of disputed texts (in the New Testament and outside its pages). An early non-Christian source may refer to women deacons in the church. Pliny the Younger, Roman governor of Bithynia about 110-112, describes his examination of Christians in order to learn the truth about their activities and says he tortured "two female slaves, who were styled women servants [ministrae, `deaconesses' ?]" (Epistles 10.96). The significance of the designation is not clear. The Latin ministrae was a general word for women servants that in this passage could refer (1) to the feminine worshipers of a deity (Christ), (2) slaves (on this meaning, perhaps Christians chose to use this term rather than slaves for their fellow believers), (3) women especially active in service (in this context Christian service), or (4) "deaconesses" (in view of the apparent reference to a special Christian usage). Being slaves, these women could not have had much independence of action on behalf of the church unless their owners were Christians.

Clement of Alexandria (about 190) may understand 1 Timothy 3:11 as "women deacons" (Miscellanies 3.6.53), but there are problems with this reference, for Clement speaks of Paul's "other

47

[second ?] letter to Timothy" (or this "other" may be in addition to the preceding reference to 1 Cor. 9:5) and many students think he refers to the enrolled widows of 1 Timothy 5:9f.

In the third century there is certain evidence for the existence of women deacons. The Syriac Didascalia 16 uses "deaconess" for a woman appointed for ministry to women, care for the sick, and assistance at the baptism of women, including instruction of these newly baptized women in pure and holy behavior. These women deacons are distinct from the widows (discussed in its preceding chapter 15) and are the counterpart of male deacons, who serve under the bishop in other matters. The name "deaconesses" was a newly coined title (the main surviving usages of the Greek word are from the fourth century)

A Speaking Role for Women in the Assembly?

In some heretical and schismatic groups of the second to fourth centuries women took prominent teaching and leading roles. This was one of the points on which writers within the mainstream of the church took exception to these groups. Tertullian (beginning of third century) was quite outspoken on this subject, as on other topics: "The very women among the heretics--what impudence! For they dare to teach, to dispute, to do exorcisms, to promise healings, perhaps also to baptize" (Prescription Against Heretics 41.5). Tertullian sometimes expressed rather negative views of women (as in On the Apparel of Women 1.1), yet he could speak appreciatively to his wife about marriage (To his Wife 2.8) and describes a believing woman's observances of times of fasting, prayer, and vigils, visiting the poor at their homes and martyrs in prison, attendance at the Lord's supper, offering hospitality to travelers, washing the feet of the saints, and providing charity (To his Wife 2.4.2). He did not speak for all in his objection to women baptizing (see above on the Didascalia 16), but by his strictures against a woman baptizing he may have meant presiding at the baptism rather than actually doing the dipping, for he links baptizing with teaching (On Baptism 1 and 17). But his views on women teaching in public were shared by the church in general. The instances of women in heretical groups taking leadership roles may not actually have been very frequent: it was the exceptional circumstances that attracted comment from the orthodox and so we know about them.

The most frequently noted example of women in a leadership role occurred among the Montanists, a movement of prophetic revival that began in Asia Minor in the third quarter of the second century. The prophetesses Priscilla and Maximilla joined Montanus as leading figures in the movement. Because of their prominence in the beginning of "the New Prophecy" (or the "Phrygian heresy," as their opponents called it), women may have continued to have a leading role. Hence, Firmilian, bishop of Caesarea in Cappadocia (mid third century), seems to refer to a Montanist when he describes a woman who in a state of ecstacy claimed to be a prophetess, for the orthodox objection to Montanist prophecy was that it was ecstatic and not rational. Firmillian says of her:

> That woman . . . among other things by which she deceived many dared frequently even this, that by an invocation not to be despised she pretended to sanctify the bread itself and to celebrate the eucharist and she offered the sacrifice to the Lord by the sacrament of the usual prayer. She also baptized many, employing the customary and proper words of interrogation so that nothing might seem different from the ecclesiastical rule. (The quotation is found in the Epistles of Cyprian 75 [74].10, to whom Firmillian wrote the letter.)

Evidently this woman consecrated the elements of the Lord's supper with the form of prayer current in catholic or mainline churches and conducted baptism according to the same formula in use in these churches. Firmillian took note because it was a woman doing it, and he concluded that she acted in this way because she was inspired by a demon. Epiphanius (fourth century) records that the Quintillianists (an offshoot of the Montanists) "have women bishops and women presbyters," in support of which they quoted Galatians 3:28 (Heresies [or Panarion] 49.2.5).

Such an exercise of leadership, especially in the assembly, may not have always been characteristic of Montanists. Tertullian, sympathetic to Montanists but no friend of a public role for women, told about a Christian sister who received ecstatic visions during "the sacred rites of the Lord's day in the church" but reported them only "after the people are dismissed at the conclusion of the sacred services" (On the Soul 9).

The Montanists justified the activities of their prophetesses by appeal to the female prophets in the Bible. The catholic or orthodox writers responded by contrasting Montanist prophecy in ecstacy with Biblical prophecy, where "the spirits of the prophets are subject to the prophets" (1 Cor. 14:32). They further made a distinction between prophetesses delivering the word of the Lord in church and doing so in other circumstances. They distinguished prophecy and other speaking roles in the assembly from those outside the assembly. Origen in the first half of the third century shows the approach:

> If the daughters of Philip prophesied, they did not speak in church, for we do not find this in the Acts of the Apostles. Neither in the old [covenant]. [Deborah, Miriam, and Huldah] did not speak in the assembly. . . . [Anna] did not speak in church. Therefore, the prophetic sign might be given for a woman to be a prophetess, but it is not permitted to her to speak in

church. . . . `Their own men' refers not only to their spouses, but [virgins and widows have] . . . a brother, kinsman, or son." (Commentary on 1 Corinthians 14:34-35)

The debate between the Montanists and their opponents in the great church is recorded in an anonymous text probably from the fourth century.[27] The orthodox Christian grants, "We do not repudiate the prophecies of women," and he mentions Mary (Luke 1:48), the daughters of Philip, and Miriam (Ex. 15:20f.). He continues with allusion to 1 Timothy 2:12, "But we do not permit them to speak in churches nor to have authority over men" (Debate of a Montanist and an Orthodox Christian, Heine, p. 125).

The presence of deviant practices in the early church is perhaps a continuation of those things which the Pauline writings opposed. The opposition to them by orthodox Christian writers shows the continued application of the Pauline prohibitions.

The common early Christian understanding of Paul's instructions is summed up in the preaching of John Chrysostom, presbyter in Antioch and later bishop of Constantinople, 398-407. Chrysostom is remembered as the greatest preacher of the ancient Greek church, and he had the education and knowledge to give him a good sense for the meaning of the words in the Greek New Testament. On 1 Corinthians 14:34-35 he has this to say:

> For if to them that have the gifts it is not permitted to speak inconsiderately, nor when they will, and this, though they be moved by the Spirit, much less to those

---

[27]Text and translation in Ronald Heine, The Montanist Oracles and Testimonia (Macon: Mercer University Press, 1989), pp. 112-127.

women who prate idly and to no purpose. . . . And if this [being in subjection] be so in respect of husbands, much more in respect of teachers and fathers and the general assemly of the church. . . . Now if they ought not to ask questions [in order to learn] much more is their speaking at pleasure contrary to law. (Homilies on 1 Corinthians 37.1)

Gregory of Nazianzus of the late fourth century paid tribute to his mother Nonna, whose husband after she converted him became a bishop and who raised her son to become known in the Greek church as "Gregory the Theologian." She excelled in piety and knowledge of the Scriptures, but "Her voice was never to be heard in the holy assemblies or holy places except in the necessary and liturgical words of the service" [the congregational "Amen" and responses in song] (Oration 18.9).

Gregory's description of Nonna's silence in church except for speaking the unison congregational words raises the question of women's participation in singing in church. There were some who applied Paul's words in 1 Corinthians 14:34 to a prohibition of singing.[28] Cyril of Jerusalem (fourth century) seems to take an intermediate view: he cited the verse in connection with his instructions that women, whose seating was segregated from the men, while preparing for baptism sing or read softly "so that their lips speak but others' ears catch not the sound" (Procatechesis 14). A prohibition of singing was not the prevailing view.

Several early writers mention that "all" sang. So that there

---

[28]Isidore of Pelusium, Epistles 1.90; Jerome, Against the Pelagians 1.25 (opposing those who advocated their singing in church).

may be no doubt that women were included, I mention some passages where they are expressly named. Philo of Alexandria, a first-century Jewish writer, described the singing of a Jewish community called the Therapeutae of which he gave a detailed account and explicitly said the singing was by "men and women alike" (The Contemplative Life 80, 83-87). Eusebius, Christian bishop of Caesarea in the early fourth century, cited Philo's account on the mistaken assumption that he was describing the early Christians and said their practice of men and women participating in responsorial singing "exactly agrees with the manner which is still observed by us" Christians (Church History 2.17.22). Ambrose, the most influential Latin bishop of the later fourth century defended women singing in church, taking into account 1 Corinthians 14:34 (On Psalm 1, Exposition 9), and elsewhere spoke of "the echo of the Psalms when sung in responsive harmony by men, women, maidens, and children" (Hexamaeron 3.5.23). John Chrysostom too specified that "men and women, old and young are distinguished according to age but are not distinguished according to the word of hymnody" (Psalms 146.2; cf. 150, "old women, men, boys, women, all who dwell on earth").

The agape (love feast) was in some respects treated differently from the assemblies for the eucharist (Lord's supper). Yet it is worth noting that the directions for observing the agape in one account include the statement: "And when they have then risen after the supper and have prayed, the children and the virgins are to say the psalms" (Apostolic Tradition 29 [25].11).

Conclusion

From the standpoint of history, the evidence of Christian writings of the second to the fourth centuries is in continuity with the New Testament. Non-canonical writings indicate women were active as Christians, not only in traditional roles of wife and mother but also in private teaching, teaching of other women, missionary work, testifying to their faith by martyrdom, and performing various service functions. Women were recognized by the church as models of asceticism as virgins and models of prayer and service as widows. In some places women were appointed as deacons to assist in ministry to women. Women were not appointed as elders, nor did they take public speaking roles in the assembly as prophets, teachers, or leaders in the assembly. Where women did take these roles in heretical and schismatic groups, this practice was a basis for objection to these groups. Although some men, like Tertullian, occasionally spoke in exaggerated disparagement of the female sex, when Christian women of the orthodox church received comment this was done in admiration.

3

DOCTRINAL CONSIDERATIONS

Were the instructions of 1 Corinthians 14 and 1 Timothy 2 about women so culturally conditioned as not meant to be universal and timeless? Were those conditions in first-century society still present in the centuries subsequent to the New Testament so that the evidence of church history may be dismissed as sharing the same cultural relativity that some assign to the New Testament? There are indications in the New Testament texts of a wider application than the culture of the first-century Mediterranean world. These indications of a doctrinal significance behind the regulations concerning women point to the decisive consideration. What really answers the question of the relevance of these texts to modern practice is doctrine. Do the teachings in 1 Corinthians 14 and 1 Timothy 2 rest on or are they in accord with fundamental Biblical doctrines? This is determinative.

So-called egalitarians find the theology of equivalence of male and female (see on Gal. 3:28 below) to overrule apparently contradictory texts. On the other side, suppose one considered 1 Corinthians 14:33 and 40 absolute and concluded that prophecy and tongue-speaking were disruptive of peace and good order in the assembly. That person might decide that 1 Corinthians 14:27-31 gave temporary concessions and that there should have been no prophecy or tongue-speaking in the assembly. What is wrong with that procedure, and how is it different from what egalitarians do with the limitations on women's speech in the assembly? Is not the proper procedure to see the detailed regulations as spelling out how the principles are to be implemented in practice? (Such is the case with Ephesians 5:21-6:9 discussed below.) The purpose of this chapter is to look at the underlying principles, the theological rationale, which gave meaning to the detailed regulations about women's activities in the assembly.

Do those texts expressing different roles for men and women actually express fundamental Christian doctrines? Paul evidently thought his directions did not rest on whim, male chauvinism, or cultural relativity but on the nature of God's created order. Moreover, that he gave doctrinal reasons for women not to teach or exercise authority in church shows that it was not culturally self-evident that they should not do so. If some women were praying, prophesying, and teaching in church, their practice indicates that they did not think there was something culturally improper in their doing so.

Let us examine the doctrinal instruction about men and women in the larger context of New Testament teachings.

The Church and the Family

The church in its organization reflects God's plan for the family. In fact, the church is described as a family. The Greek word oikos may refer to a house, a dwelling place, a building; and in this sense on occasion refers to the dwelling place of deity, a temple. The word also may refer to those who dwell in a house, the household or family. Sometimes it is difficult to classify a given

56

passage, but the reference to people tilts the meaning toward family or household in the following passages, even if connotations of the people as a spiritual temple are also present: "I am writing these instructions to you so that . . . you may know how one ought to behave in the household of God, which is the church of the living God" (1 Tim. 3:14-15, particularly significant as immediately following the directions about women in chapter 2 and about a bishop and deacons in chapter 3); "Now Moses was faithful in all God's house as a servant . . .; Christ, however, was faithful over God's house as a son, and we are his house" (Heb. 3:5-6); "For the time has come for judgment to begin with the household of God" (1 Pet. 4:17).

In the family that functions according to God's regulations the husband exercises a loving headship or leadership. This pattern of relationship was established at least as early as Genesis 3:16, where the husband is said to "rule over" the wife. Paul stated the relationship still to be in effect under the new covenant of Christ: "I want you to understand that Christ is the head of every man, and the husband is the head of his wife, and God is the head of Christ" (1 Cor. 11:3).

The household codes of the New Testament reflect the instructions that Greco-Roman philosophers and moralists gave for household relationships, but infuse these relationships with a Christian perspective. "Wives, submit yourselves to your husbands [that much the pagan writers said], as is fitting in the Lord [the distinctly Christian motivation]. Husbands, love your wives [going beyond ruling over them] and never treat them harshly [the manner of the leadership]" (Col. 3:18-19). Wives are not told to obey, but to "submit yourselves" or "be submissive"; children and slaves are told to "obey" (Col. 3:18, 20, 22; same in Eph. 5:24,; 6:1, 5). "Wives, in the same way [the pattern of submission, like that of slaves for masters, was set by Christ's example--2:18-25], accept the authority of [be submissive to] your own husbands . . . . Husbands, in the same way, show consideration [honor] to the feminine weaker vessel, [but here also an affirmation of equal worth] since they too are co-heirs of the grace of life" (1 Pet. 3:1-7).

The fullest statement of husband-wife relationships in the New Testament occurs in Ephesians 5:21-33. The passage is part of a whole section that spells out how mutual submission (5:21) expresses itself in various household relationships (continuing through 6:9). For wives submission means "submitting themselves to their own husbands as to the Lord" (5:22, again the distinctively Christian version of the relationship). For husbands submission means "love your wives as also Christ loved the church and gave himself up for her" (5:25), a very high demand indeed. The passage presents the relationship of Christ and the church as the pattern for the husband-wife relationship: "as to the Lord" and "as Christ loved." Note the conclusion, "This [marriage] is a great mystery, and I am applying it to Christ and the church. Each of you, however, should love his wife as himself, and a wife should respect her husband" (Eph. 5:32-33). The verses in Ephesians 5 quite clearly, but also Colossians 3 and 1 Peter 3, show the husband's headship to be based on love. Loving service (as shown by Christ) calls forth loving obedience. The husband is never told to command obedience from the wife. The husband's headship is not arbitrary or dictatorial, and the wife's submission is voluntary, not enforced.

Any social group has to have some form of leadership. This applies to the smallest and most basic unit of human society, the family.   In the family this leadership is assigned to the husband/father. Not every male, just because of reaching an age of accountability, is given authority in a family (see Luke 2:42, 51)--the same is true for the church.

Leadership in the church corresponds to leadership in the family. As indicated above, the leadership in the family derives from the pattern set by Christ and the church. Since the church is a family, we should expect the same principles of organization to be operative in the church as apply to the family, and indeed this is true. Leadership in the church is given to male family heads, not to all males. The qualifications for bishops/elders exclude women from this position: "Now a bishop must be . . . the husband of one wife . . . . He must manage his own household [oikos] well, having his children in submission with all dignity--for if someone does not know how to manage his own household [oikos], how can he take care of God's church [ekklēsia]?" (1 Tim. 3:2, 4-5). "Appoint elders in every town . . . someone who is the husband of one wife, whose children are believers, not accused of debauchery and not rebellious" (Tit. 1:5-6).   Elders are stewards administering the affairs of God's household (Tit. 1:7). They gain experience for this position from their own family life.

The pattern of male leadership was set for the church at the beginning. When the Twelve (apostles), themselves men, gave directions for appointing the Seven, they instructed the congregation (adelphoi, probably in the inclusive sense of "brothers and sisters") to search out men (andras) to be put in charge of the relief of widows (Acts 6:3). The choice was made by "the whole community," apparently men and women, but all those chosen were men (Acts 6:5).

The teachings given in the New Testament in regard to the assembly are in accord with what is said about the church's organization. As the leadership of the church (elders) is given to men, so leadership in that which expresses what the church is, namely its assembly, is exercised by men. Moreover, the nature of the church as a family is reflected in the assembly. The gathered church reflects its nature as the family or household of God. It comes together in the presence of God according to God's arrangements for the family. As the husband in the family exercises a leadership of love, so in the church its elders acting as stewards of God's household exercise a loving, serving leadership following the example of Jesus (Matt. 20:25-28; John 13:1-17; 1 Pet. 5:2-4). God's ranking of male and female going back to the creation and fall (see the next section) is reflected in males taking the leadership in the assembly and females following this leadership in respectful silence.

In view of what is said in the New Testament about leadership in the family, what is said about the organization of the church is only what should be expected. Likewise, in view of the teachings given about the organization of the church in 1 Timothy 3 and Titus 1, the instructions about women's role in the assembly in 1 Corinthians 14 and 1 Timothy 2 are only what should be expected.

The Created Order

Male-Female relations are based on the created order. Passages about women in the church examined in chapter 1 ground their teaching on the nature of God and the relationships he established at creation--1 Corinthians 11:9, 11-12; 14:33-34;

1Timothy 2:13-15. Sometimes interpreters, positing an egalitarian reading of Genesis 1-2, make that the basis for interpreting Paul's theology instead of letting Paul's understanding of Genesis guide the interpretation of Paul's teaching. Rather than deciding from Genesis what one thinks Paul should have said, one ought to let Paul express how he read Genesis. Paul leaves us in no doubt of his ranking of male and female (1 Cor. 11:3--God, Christ, man, woman). Other passages show an equality of Christ with God in their divine nature (John 1:1; Phil. 2:6; Col. 1:15-17), but a functional difference is seen in the incarnation. An equality of nature did not contradict a difference in function. Paul affirms a priority for the male and a mutuality for male and female but never an equality of functions.

Genesis 1-3 presents 3 basic ideas in regard to men and women: an affirmation of sexuality, the equality of the sexes, and differences of function for the sexes. Genesis 1:26-27 establishes the sexual distinction of male and female and the fundamental equality of human beings, male and female, all made in the image of God. The image of God in human beings is the basis for their ruling over creation (Gen. 1:26).

Genesis 2:7, 18-23 establishes a difference of function and status for the woman as derived from the man. The male is first, and God addresses Adam as the representative human being. Eve was created second (from Adam, not from earth); she was designated his helper; and Adam named her after himself (man--woman). "Helper" (Gen. 2:18) is "one who gives help or support," in this case a companion complementary to the man. Hence, there is a mutual relationship resulting from the undesirability of man being alone. No subordination is implied, but the word does affirm the purpose for woman. Women know how much we men need help! "Naming" is more indicative of male leadership. For the significance of giving a name note Psalm 147:4 and Isaiah 43:1 and of wearing someone's name Isaiah 63:19; 4:1. In Genesis 2-3 God addresses Adam, not Eve. Although some read too much into these facts, they do present the woman in a secondary position.

Genesis 3:16 establishes (or reinforces) a condition of subordination for woman as a consequence of sin. The fall disrupted the mutuality between male and female intended at creation. Genesis 3:16 is not proof that subordination is a punishment for the fall, but it does indicate an intensification of the relationship of man and woman. That men abuse their position is an expression of the fall. Even if the hierarchy of male and female is totally the result of the fall, we still live in the fallen world and full restoration to the ideal of creation must await the consummation of redemption. God addressed Eve with the words, "I will greatly increase your pangs in childbearing; in pain you shall bring forth children, yet your desire shall be for your husband, and he shall rule over you" (Gen. 3:16). The coming of Christ and the redemption from sin he brought has not canceled the pain involved in childbirth nor the sexual attraction of female and male; nor has it canceled God's order of the rule of husband over wife (the manner of its exercise is changed). Paul, however, understood a hierarchical relation of male and female to have existed from before the fall, from the creation of male and female--1 Corinthians11:3,11-12; 1 Timothy 2:13.

Why is a distinction made in regard to the assembly that is not made elsewhere? Why is a distinction made between in and out of the assembly? There is a direct correlation made between the family and the church, but there might not seem immediately to be such a connection between creation and the assembly of the church. In the absence of an explicit explanation, I can only draw an inference from what is said. The assembly brings God's people into his presence in a special way and so is meant to reflect the character of God and what he instituted at creation. Man and woman have distinctive spheres in which to show their identity as male and female, and one of these finds expression in the meeting of the church. The leaders in the assembly are representatives of God to the people and of the people to God. As representatives of God, they are men. God transcends sexual distinctions, but most often he represents himself by male imagery--Father, King, etc. Christ became incarnate as male. Hence, those who bring God's word, who speak for God in the assembly, are men. The representatives of the congregation bring the words of the people to God. Since the church is a family and the man is given headship in the family, this representative role is given to men. This explanation is my hypothesis; someone else may offer a better explanation. The differences of function assigned to men and women are fact.

These doctrinal affirmations based on the created order may find some support from anthropological, sociological, and psychological studies.[29] Through history most human societies have expected male leadership and have made some general distinctions between male and female spheres of activity. How male headship is understood and how the division of labor between male and female is assigned vary considerably from one society to another, as does the degree of distinction between men and women that is

---

[29]Werner Neuer, Man and Woman in Christian Perspective (Wheaton: Crossway, 1991), especially pp. 23-56.

made. The division of tasks is sometimes quite arbitrary and seldom absolute within a culture, as well as varying from one culture to another. Modern "western" societies have modified their traditional practices considerably. Culture and environment greatly influence human behavior from birth, so it is disputed whether psychological distinctions that are often made between the sexes have any basis in biological and physiological differences and if so to what extent. Nor is it evident that the societal distinctions that have prevailed through history derive from biological differences that go beyond the obvious anatomical differences between the sexes. Adherence to Biblical principles about the relationships of men and women is not dependent on being able to demonstrate by scientific study that these principles are embedded in the created nature of male and female. What men and women have in common is greater than their differences, but that men and women are created at a minimum with physiological/anatomical differences shows that God has different purposes for them. We may be solely dependent on revelation for determining what these purposes are. Whatever distinctive characteristics of men and women beyond their biological differences that may be established do not mean one sex is inferior to the other, only that they are different. Distortions of the differences and of male-female relationships came from the fall; the distinctions themselves do not.

Oneness in Christ--Galatians 3:28

The crucial text for those who seek Biblical warrant for giving women equality with men in the leadership of the church is Galatians 3:28, "There is neither Jew nor Greek, there is neither slave nor free, there is neither male and female; for all of you are one in Christ

Jesus." The unity of male and female as equally made in the image of God that is stated in Genesis 1:27 is here (re)affirmed as realized in Christ. This charter verse of racial, social, and gender equality in Christ, however, does not abolish all the differences and least of all the differences of function between male and female.

In its context Galatians 3:28 has to do with admission to the people of God and one's status before God. Paul is arguing against Judaizers who wanted to bind circumcision and certain features of the Law of Moses on Gentile converts. He insists that the law of Moses was temporary and that now through faith and baptism all have equal access to the promises made to Abraham and his descendants (Gal. 3:23-29). Paul's statement contrasts with the regulations of many (not all) Greek sanctuaries that prohibited admission to foreigners, slaves, and women (note the order).

The three pairs of Galatians 3:28 likely derive from the covenant of circumcision in Genesis 17:9-14. The first persons in each pair were subject to circumcision; in contrast all receive baptism into the Christian community. Although all have full standing in the community, their unity was not uniformity of social roles and obligations. Diversity pertaining to these distinctions remains (so Paul affirms in 1 Corinthians 7:17-24), so there was no conflict between Galatians 3:28 and the household (or station) codes like Colossians 3:18-4:1.[30]

Many, however, take Galatians 3:28 as a formula associated

---

[30]Troy W. Martin, "The Covenant of Circumcision (Genesis 17:9-14) and the Situational Antitheses in Galatians 3:28," Journal of Biblical Literatuare 122 (2003): 111-125.

with baptism (cf. 1 Corinthians 12:13; Colossians 3:11). If so, does the principle stated have wider implications for community life beyond the conditions of admission to the community?

The principle of oneness certainly has something to do with how Christians treat one another (1 Cor. 12:25-26). But being one in Christ does not abolish differences. "The body is one," but it "has many members" (1 Cor. 12:12) that are quite different (1 Cor. 12:14-30). The members of the body are equal and all necessary, but they do not have the same functions. Although our human body is one, "not all the members [of that body] have the same function" (Rom. 12:4); the same is true for the body of Christ (Rom. 12:5-8). Being one in Christ does not abolish different functions for male and female and the different instructions that pertain to those different functions. When a person takes these parallels about oneness in Christ into account, then Galatians 3:28 rather than declaring identity, if anything, supports different functions while affirming equal status before God.

On becoming a Christian one does not cease being circumcised or uncircumcised (a Jew or a Gentile), slave or free (1 Cor. 7:17-24). In a society where slavery exists, the regulations for masters and slaves would still apply (Col. 3:22-4:1), but the presence of those regulations in the New Testament (written at a time when slavery was a common social institution and generally accepted) does not require the continuation of this social relationship. When society comes to realize (and this occurred under the influence of Christian principles) that the condition of slavery is wrong and the institution no longer exists, then of course the separate instructions to masters and slaves are no longer directly applicable.

Just as a person in Christ continues to be a Jew or a Gentile, slave or free, so one does not cease being male and female. Unlike slavery, a changeable human institution, but like being born a Jew or a Gentile, a person's gender is not subject to change (not naturally--that one can undergo a sex change operation does not affect the argument here any more than does a Gentile becoming circumcised or a Jew having an operation to remove his circumcision). The normal biological, psychological, and sociological differences between male and female remain, and so do the regulations pertaining to their different roles (Eph. 5:22-33).

The abolition of male-female differences is an eschatological condition. As Jesus said in refuting those who denied a bodily resurrection:

> Those who belong to this age marry and are given in marriage; but those who are considered worthy of a place in that age and in the resurrection from the dead neither marry nor are given in marriage. Indeed they cannot die anymore, because they are like angels and are children of God, being children of the resurrection.
> (Luke 20:34-36)

It is a mistake to try to anticipate that condition in this life. That mistake was apparently being made by some Corinthian Christains (1 Cor. 4:8) and may have been behind their rejection of sexual relations that called forth the regulations of 1 Corinthians 7. Again, we note that Paul's addressing a specific situation does not relativize his teaching on marriage. Others claimed that the resurrection had already occurred (2 Tim. 2:18), and that may have been behind the forbidding of marriage (1 Tim. 4:3). The presence of such teachings in the same letters giving limitations on women's public leadership in the church may be indicative of a correlation between the ideas of

67

living the resurrection life now and the removal of restrictions on women's public role in the church. Whatever the circumstances, the principles enunciated in response to the problems remain valid. We still live in "this age," not in the age of the physical resurrection.

Some Implications of the Doctrines

The doctrines of the church as a family, the created order of nature, and spiritual (not physical) oneness in the body of Christ undergird the New Testament injunctions about different male and female functions and about male leadership and female submission in the church.

Different roles, however, do not imply superiority or inferiority in worth. A person's role and that person's worth are not related in Scripture. A bold and striking demonstration of this truth is Christ himself. Although being in the form of God, he took the form of a slave (Phil. 2:6-7). He not only had the worth but even the form of God. Yet he took on the function of the Servant, even a slave. This assumption of the role of a slave did not diminish his worth; if anything, it enhanced it. According to his teaching and example, the role of a servant makes one great in the kingdom of heaven (Matt. 20:20-28; Mark 10:35-45; Luke 22:24-27). The serving functions are the path to greatness in the kingdom of God.

Limitations on women's role in the assembly and functional distinctions between men and women, morever, imply no inferiority of women's ability. Any given woman may be the spiritual superior of any given man. Silence in the assembly does not mean inferiority and should not be interpreted to mean this. I happily acknowledge the influence of many spiritual women in my life, and I readily defer to their spiritual insight and judgment on many matters.

Equality is not the same as identity, and differences of the sexes do not mean inequality. Male domination and female equivalence with the male are both distortions of God's intention in creation.

The wide acceptance in western societies today that the sexes have equal value is largely to be ascribed to the influence of Christianity. One may readily contrast the condition of women in societies where the influence of Christianity is minimal or non-existent, as in primitive societies and those dominated by another religion. I can remember when I was young that the treatment of women was listed as one of the arguments in the apologetic for the truth of Christianity. Today there is the opposite situation where many blame what is regarded as a suppression of women on the Bible and Christianity. However, their desire to take equality of worth to mean identity and to abrogate a difference of roles for men and women is possible only from an initial premise of the equality of men and women. And for that principle modern societies are indebted to Christianity and the Biblical principle of male and female created in the image of God.

The theological reasons discussed above show that the Biblical view of women was not simply derived from culture, even if influenced by it. For instance, there were many women priests in the ancient Near East and (as noted in chapter 2) in the Greco-Roman world, but not in Israel. The culturally acceptable practice would have been for Israel to have priestesses. The fact that there were women prophets in the Old Testament makes all the more notable that there were no women priests. It would not have been unheard of for the church to put women in positions of official leadership, which they held in Greco-Roman civil and religious life. Women of wealth, social status, and/or ability no doubt had much influence in the church, as they did in Israel, in Greco-Roman society, and as they still do today in society and church. But influence is not the same as appointment to recognized functions.

As another indication that something more than culture was involved, one may note the example of Jesus. Jesus broke with culture in his treatment of women. For instance, the Gospels record his close relationships with women, his tender treatment of them, and even his teaching and entering into religious discussions with them. He welcomed women to be instructed by him, as Martha and Mary (Luke 10:38-42) and the Samaritan woman at the well (John 4:27), contrary to rabbinic practice. Jesus equalized divorce law, forbidding the man as well as the woman to initiate a divorce, contrary to Jewish precedent (Mark 10:11-12). These breaks with convention show that Jesus' selection of men for the Twelve was deliberate.

Sometimes interpreters point to Jesus' treatment of women as an indication that he did not want limitations placed on their service but then argue that it was because of cultural considerations that he chose only men as apostles and his apostles in turn placed restrictions on women's activities. However, one cannot have it both ways, as if Jesus were a counter-cultural egalitarian and the restrictions on women were cultural. If Jesus broke with cultural conventions in some regards, he and his apostles could have in others, such as the choice of the Twelve or in the qualifications of elders. If Jesus departed from cultural conventions in his treatment of women, and that seems to be indicated by the texts, then feminists and egalitarians have no case for New Testament teachings being determined by the culture and thus irrelevant to us today.

Some Practical Applications

The Biblical instructions, supported by historical evidence and sanctioned by important doctrinal premises, would exclude women from preaching, teaching, and leading in prayer in the assemblies of the church. The close association of song with prayer (many songs are prayer songs, and note their connection in 1 Cor. 14:15) and with teaching (many songs are exhortations; see the connection in Col. 3:16) would seem to require that the limitations on woman's public role be extended to include song leading.

The limitations do not apply to teaching of other women and children, as in Bible classes or other small groups. If a church in a given place is composed only of women and children or if there is a meeting of only women, then of course the women take the lead. If there are only a few men in the congregation and those incapable, my judgment would be that the women in a modest and unassertive manner should take the lead; this would be an interim arrangement until such time as men could fill their God-appointed roles. The serving of communion, since it is a serving role--in contrast to presiding, making a talk, or leading in prayer--would seem to be open to women. Where serving the elements is perceived as itself an act of leadership, then this role becomes problematic.

Nor do the limitations apply to secondary or derivative

speaking or leadership roles. For example, signing for the deaf the words of a lesson, prayer, or song delivered or led by another does not involve speaking at all. In a comparable way, acting as a translator or interpreter for a speaker of another language to people who do not understand the language would not be delivering her own message but transmitting the message of another. Confessing one's faith at baptism in response to the questions put by the one presiding at the baptism would not violate the prohibition on speaking.

Some activities would have to fall in the category of opinion, where the judgment of one congregation might differ from that of another congregation. In my opinion, the individual public reading of the Scripture lesson(s) would be among the excluded actions. Although not "teaching" in the sense of interpreting and applying Scripture, this act is still a form of bringing the word of God to people, something forbidden to women in 1 Corinthians 14:29-35 and 1 Timothy 2:11-12.

The Biblical limitations on women's activities are addressed to the church and not to their place in society at large (business, professions, education, politics, etc.). The absence of limitations in those spheres, however, would not mean that every activity would be wise for a Christian woman.

Paul in 1 Corinthians 14:19, 28, 34-35 (cf. 1 Cor. 11:18, 33-34) makes a distinction between activities "at home" (en oikos) and "in church [assembly]" (en ekklesia). Most Christians do not have a problem with making a distinction between the home--in which women may lead in prayer, lead in song, and teach visitors and other members of the family, including the husband--and the

72

church assembled, where the men take the leading roles.

There will be church meetings that are not regular assemblies but when the church is acting in a church capacity. Such would include evangelistic services ("gospel meetings"), meetings to determine church discipline (Matt. 18:17-20; 1 Cor. 5:3-5), or baptisms. On these occasions the church will conduct its service in the manner it would its other assemblies. What then about Bible classes, "care groups," and other small group activities? In these there is not the intention that "the whole church comes together" (1 Cor. 14:23), nor are they a family or strictly a "home" activity, for they may have a church sponsorship or endorsement. One can make the case that these gatherings are extensions of the assembly and are church activities and therefore the same teachings should apply to them as to the assembly. On the other hand, there is a need for occasions when women and men speak, discuss, and ask questions. Each congregation needs to decide for itself, while being respectful of Biblical principles, what its policy will be in regard to any given situation.

Christian educational enterprises at the elementary, secondary, and college/university levels normally include chapel services. Are these "church," or are they something different? Since the chapel or religious exercises represent the church side of the school's life, they should reflect church practice. It is also appropriate that a distinction be made, even if it appears arbitrary, between the devotional exercises and the other activities in the schools' assemblies.

Difficulties in making distinctions in a congregational, educational, or any other setting does not mean no distinction is to be made. Any time judgments have to made there is a danger of inconsistency or perceived inconsistency. Nonetheless, Christians will strive for faithfulness and consistency, all the time acting in humility and charity.

To help in making decisions in regard to "intermediate" or unclear situations, some guidelines may be offered. Does the meeting represent the church as church (1 Cor. 11:18)? If so, the rules for the church should be followed. Some activities are an expression of the assembled church; others are not. Another, related, question is, What is the intention of the meeting? Not every group activity by Christians is "church," nor is it intended to be (for example, getting together for a purely social activity). The reverse side of this question is, How is the activity perceived by others? Weddings and funerals are not explicitly church gatherings, but the religious element will for Christians be prominent. In all such cases good judgment must be used and tolerance respected.

Concluding Remarks

The doctrinal points in the New Testament texts indicate that God's plan for the home and the church is male leadership. This involves men in the position of bishops/elders and men leading in the activities of the assembly of the church--taking the individual speaking roles in presiding, preaching, teaching, praying, and praising. Male spiritual leadership is based on God's design going back to creation and still in effect in the beginning of the new creation in Christ. The full realization of oneness in Christ, including the elimination of sexual differences, will not occur until the resurrection life is completed in the world to come.

According to the New Testament, some activities in the assembly are forbidden to women--bringing the word of God to the people (whether in teaching, edification, exhortation, or consolation), acting as representative of the church (as in leading of prayer), or assuming the leadership of the assembly (leading of singing and presiding over the meeting as a whole or parts thereof, like the Lord's supper). Some activities would seem to be allowed--group or corporate activities and serving functions when these are not themselves viewed as leadership roles. Some activities are not clearly in one category or the other; in these cases different circumstances may call for different practices and opinions may differ--if something is to be done, it is to be done in the spirit of Biblical principles for male/female roles and with respect for the conscience of others and so as to preserve unity.

Leadership functions by men imply no "secondary status" for women in the kingdom. Jesus' own example gives priority to the serving functions (Matt. 20:25-28). Apart from the few more prominent leadership activities, which in kingdom terms are actually "inferior" activities, women were fully involved in advancing the gospel, teaching and training others, leading in benevolence, and doing all the things necessary for the welfare and spiritual life of others.

Christians want to answer the questions posed by others and to accommodate the culture in which they find themselves as much as possible. The decisive question for a Christian, however, is never how one answers the ideological questions of the time, as important as that might be for apologetical purposes. The crucial consideration is how to be obedient to the will of God.

"Heresies increased greatly because those who received them were unwilling to learn the mind of the apostles, but followed only their own desires, doing what pleased them and not what was right." (Apostolic Tradition 43.3, Arabic version)

Everett Ferguson

Everett Ferguson was born in Montgomery, Texas, and grew up in El Campo, Texas. After receiving B.A. (valedictorian) and M.A. degrees from Abilene Christian University, he earned the S.T.B. (top student) and PhD. ("With Distinction") degrees from Harvard University. At Harvard he was an Honorary John Harvard Fellow and the graduate assistant to A.D. Nock in the history of religions. Ferguson was the first Dean at Northeastern Christian Junior College. Then he taught from 1962 until his retirement in 1998 at Abilene Christian University, where he was twice teacher of the year (once in the College of Liberal and Fine Arts and once in the College of Biblical Studies) and for a time Director of Graduate Studies in Bible.

Ferguson is a member of several professional societies: Society of Biblical Literature, American Society of Church History (member of the council, 1983-1985), North American Patristics Society (president, 1990-1992), Ecclesiastical History Society (Great Britain),Association international d''etudes patristiques (member of the council, 1995-), and Conference on Faith and History. He has been active in the Institute for Biblical Research. The Southwest Commission for Religious Studies selected him as its John G.Gammie Senior Lecturer for 1996-1997. Colleagueshonored him with a Festschrift--<u>The Early Church in Its Context: Essays in Honor of Everett Ferguson</u>, ed. Abraham J. Malherbe, Frederick W. Norris, & James W. Thompson (Leiden: E.J. Brill, 1998)--and with a special issue of *Restoration Quarterly*, Volume 40.1 (1998).

Extensive travels include study trips to Greece, Israel, Turkey and Egypt. Ferguson has taught courses at Wembley (London) Bible School, Southern Africa Bible School, Nigerian Christian Bible

College, Athens International Bible Institute, Great Lakes Bible College, and South Pacific Bible College.   He has lectured at Harding University, York College, Great Lakes Christian College, Pepperdine University, Collegio Biblico, Cincinnati Bible Seminary, Ohio Valley College, Oklahoma Christian University, Freed-Hardeman University, Faulkner University, Southwestern Baptist Theological Seminary, University of Pretoria, Mutare Bible College (Zimbabwe), Austin Graduate School of Theology, Bible College of New Zealand (Tauranga), Carey Baptist College (Auckland, New Zealand), Australian Catholic University (Brisbane), and University of Melbourne.

Ferguson has been invited to preach and give special lectures in churches in the United States and abroad. He served over twenty years as an elder of the Hillcrest Church of Christ in Abilene, Texas.

His wife Nancy is a Bible class teacher, lecturer at women's programs, and an author.   They have three children and five grandchildren. They reside in Abilene, Texas

Publications

Eight volumes in the Way of Life series:
Church History: Early and Medieval. Abilene: Biblical Research Press, 1966
Church History: Reformation and Modern. Abilene: Biblical Research Press, 1967. Both now ACU Press
New Testament Church. Abilene: Biblical Research Press, 1968. Now ACU Press
A Cappella Music in the Public Worship of the Church. Abilene: Biblical Research Press, 1972. Third edition, Fort Worth: Star Bible Publications, 1999

The Letters of John. Message of the New Testament. Abilene: Biblical Research Press, 1984.

Acts of the Apostles. 2 Volumes. Message of the New Testament. Abilene: ACU Press, 1986. Reprint, Henderson, TN: Hester Publications, 2003.

The Everlasting Kingdom. Abilene: ACU Press, 1989.

Full length books:

Early Christians Speak. Austin: Sweet, 1971. Third edition, Abilene: ACU Press, 1999

Early Christians Speak, Volume 2, Abilene: ACU Press, 2002

Gregory of Nyssa: Life of Moses. With A.J. Malherbe. New York: Paulist Press, 1978.

Demonology of the Early Christian World. New York: Edwin Mellen, 1985.

Backgrounds of Early Christianity. Grand Rapids: Eerdmans, 1987. Third edition, 2003.

The Church of Christ: A Biblical Ecclesiology for Today. Grand Rapids: Eerdmans, 1996. Translated into Korean, 1997.

Works edited:

Living Word Commentary on the New Testament. 19 volumes in 23 parts. Austin: Sweet, 1967-1979. Now Abilene: ACU Press.

Christian Teaching: Studies in Honor of LeMoine G. Lewis. Abilene. ACU Bookstore, 1981.

The Second Century: A Journal of Early Christian Studies. 1981-1992

Restoration Quarterly. 1987-1992.

Encyclopedia of Early Christianity. New York: Garland, 1990. Second edition, 1997.

Studies in Early Christianity. 18 volumes. New York: Garland, 1993

Journal of Early Christian Studies. Co-editor. 1993-1999

Recent Studies in Early Christianity. 6 volumes New York: Garland, 1999.

Consulting editor for *Eerdmans Dictionary of the Bible* (2000) and *Encyclopedia of the Stone-Campbell Movement* (2004)

Articles

Articles and book reviews have appeared in such scholarly journals as *Harvard Theological Review*, *Journal of Ecclesiastical History*, *Theologische Zeitschrift*, *Church History*, *Ekklesiastikos Pharos*, *Greek Orthodox Theological Review*, *Journal of Theological Studies*, *Scottish Journal of Theology*, and *Studia Patristica*.